Fabulous '50s
RECIPE COLLECTION

Publications International, Ltd.

Favorite Brand Name Recipes at www.fbnr.com

Pictured on the front cover: Escalloped Chicken *(page 110).*

Pictured on the back cover *(top to bottom):* Hickory Beef Kabob *(page 81),* Browned Pork Chop with Gravy *(page 42)* and Brownie Baked Alaska *(page 187).*

ISBN: 1-4127-0181-3

Library of Congress Control Number: 2003113367

Manufactured in China.

8 7 6 5 4 3 2 1

Microwave Cooking: Microwave ovens vary in wattage. Use the cooking times as guidelines and check for doneness before adding more time.

Preparation/Cooking Times: Preparation times are based on the approximate amount of time required to assemble the recipe before cooking, baking, chilling or serving. These times include preparation steps such as measuring, chopping and mixing. The fact that some preparations and cooking can be done simultaneously is taken into account. Preparation of optional ingredients and serving suggestions is not included.

Table of Contents

Parties & Cocktails

Start your party with in-vogue nibbles like cheese puffs, stuffed mushrooms and mini meatballs. In the '50s, "dips were hip." Try California and clam dip— they're still all the rage.

The Famous Lipton® California Dip

The Famous Lipton® California Dip

1 envelope LIPTON® RECIPE SECRETS® Onion Soup Mix
1 container (16 ounces) regular or light sour cream

1. In medium bowl, blend all ingredients; chill at least 2 hours.

2. Serve with your favorite dippers.   ***Makes about 2 cups dip***

Tip: For a creamier dip, add more sour cream.

Sensational Spinach Dip: Add 1 package (10 ounces) frozen chopped spinach, thawed and squeezed dry.

California Seafood Dip: Add 1 cup finely chopped cooked clams, crabmeat or shrimp, ¼ cup chili sauce and 1 tablespoon horseradish.

California Bacon Dip: Add ⅓ cup crumbled cooked bacon or bacon bits.

California Blue Cheese Dip: Add ¼ pound crumbled blue cheese and ¼ cup finely chopped walnuts.

Mini Cocktail Meatballs

1 envelope LIPTON® RECIPE SECRETS® Onion, Onion
**   Mushroom, Beefy Mushroom or Beefy Onion Soup Mix**
1 pound ground beef
½ cup plain dry bread crumbs
¼ cup dry red wine or water
2 eggs, lightly beaten

Preheat oven to 375°F.

In medium bowl, combine all ingredients; shape into 1-inch meatballs.

In shallow baking pan, arrange meatballs and bake 18 minutes or until done. Serve, if desired, with assorted mustards or tomato sauce.

Makes about 4 dozen meatballs

Devilish Crab Puffs

Swiss Puffs (recipe follows)
2 cups crabmeat, cleaned
¼ cup chopped fresh parsley
¼ cup mayonnaise
2 tablespoons finely minced onion
2 teaspoons white wine
1 teaspoon dry mustard
1 teaspoon lemon juice
1 teaspoon Worcestershire sauce
¼ teaspoon white pepper

1. Prepare Swiss Puffs; set aside.

2. To make filling, place crabmeat in medium bowl. Add parsley, mayonnaise, onion, wine, mustard, lemon juice, Worcestershire and pepper. Stir gently to blend.

3. Preheat oven to 375°F. Fill Swiss Puffs with crab filling.

4. Place filled appetizers on *ungreased* baking sheets; bake 10 minutes or until heated through. ***Makes about 40 appetizers***

Swiss Puffs

½ cup milk
½ cup water
¼ cup butter or margarine
¼ teaspoon salt
  Pinch white pepper
  Pinch ground nutmeg
1 cup all-purpose flour
4 eggs, at room temperature
1 cup shredded Swiss cheese, divided

1. Preheat oven to 400°F.

2. Heat milk, water, butter, salt, pepper and nutmeg in 3-quart saucepan over medium-high heat until mixture boils. Remove pan from heat; add flour, mixing until smooth. Cook over medium-low heat, stirring constantly, until mixture leaves side of pan clean and forms a ball. Remove pan from heat.

3. Add eggs, 1 at a time, beating until smooth and shiny after each addition. Continue beating until mixture loses its gloss. Stir in ¾ cup cheese.

4. Drop rounded teaspoonfuls of cheese batter 1 inch apart onto 2 large greased baking sheets. Sprinkle with remaining ¼ cup cheese.

5. Bake 30 to 35 minutes or until puffs are golden brown. Cool completely on wire racks.

6. Before filling, cut tops off puffs; scoop out and discard moist dough in centers.   **Makes about 4 dozen**

Devilish Crab Puffs

Nutty Bacon Cheeseball

  1 package (8 ounces) cream cheese, softened
½ cup milk
  2 cups (8 ounces) shredded sharp Cheddar cheese
  2 cups (8 ounces) shredded Monterey Jack cheese
¼ cup (1 ounce) crumbled blue cheese
¼ cup finely minced green onions (white parts only)
  1 jar (2 ounces) diced pimento, drained
10 slices bacon, cooked, drained, finely crumbled and divided
¾ cup finely chopped pecans, divided
    Salt and black pepper to taste
¼ cup minced parsley
  1 tablespoon poppy seeds

Beat cream cheese and milk on low speed in large bowl with electric mixer until blended. Add cheeses. Blend on medium speed until well combined. Add green onions, pimento, half of bacon and half of pecans. Blend on medium speed until well mixed. Add salt and pepper to taste. Transfer half of mixture to large piece of plastic wrap. Form into ball; wrap tightly. Repeat with remaining mixture. Refrigerate until chilled, at least two hours.

Combine remaining bacon and pecans with parsley and poppy seeds in pie plate or large dinner plate. Remove plastic wrap from each ball; roll each in bacon mixture until well coated. Wrap each ball tightly in plastic wrap and refrigerate until ready to use, up to 24 hours.

Makes about 24 servings

Parties & Cocktails

Nutty Bacon Cheeseball

Molded Crab Mousse

2 cans (6 ounces each) crab meat *or* 2 cups fresh shelled crab meat
1 cup (4 ounces) shredded Colby cheese
½ cup finely chopped celery
¼ cup finely chopped onion
¼ cup finely chopped red bell pepper
¼ cup finely chopped green bell pepper
1 cup sour cream
½ cup mayonnaise
¼ cup chili sauce
2 tablespoons fresh lemon juice
3 tablespoons cold water
1 tablespoon unflavored gelatin
Cucumber slices (optional)
Fresh dill sprigs (optional)

1. Lightly oil 1-quart fish-shaped or other shaped mold.

2. Place crab meat in large bowl. Toss with cheese, celery, onion and bell peppers.

3. Combine sour cream, mayonnaise, chili sauce and lemon juice in small bowl. Pour cold water into small saucepan; stir in gelatin. Cook over low heat, stirring constantly, until thoroughly dissolved. Stir quickly into sour cream mixture.

4. Fold sour cream mixture into crab mixture; spoon into prepared mold. Cover with plastic wrap; refrigerate 3 hours or until set. Unmold onto serving platter. Garnish with cucumber slices and dill sprigs, if desired.

Makes 32 appetizer servings (2 tablespoons each)

Cheddar Cheese Puffs

PUFFS
- 1 cup water
- 6 tablespoons butter, cut into pieces
- 1 teaspoon salt
- Pepper to taste
- Ground nutmeg (optional)
- 1 cup all-purpose flour
- 5 eggs, divided
- 1 cup plus 3 tablespoons finely shredded Cheddar or Swiss cheese, divided

FILLING
- 1 (11-ounce) jar NEWMAN'S OWN® All Natural Salsa
- 12 ounces cream cheese, softened

Preheat oven to 425°F. In heavy 2-quart saucepan, place water, butter, salt, pepper and nutmeg. When butter has melted and water is boiling, remove from heat. With wooden spoon, beat in flour all at once. (If mixture does not form a ball and leave the sides of pan clean, return to medium heat and beat vigorously for 1 to 2 minutes.) Remove from heat and beat in 4 eggs, 1 at a time, until each egg is thoroughly blended. Beat in 1 cup cheese. Place in pastry bag with ½-inch-diameter round tip and pipe 1-inch rounds on 2 greased baking sheets. Beat remaining egg. Brush tops of puffs with beaten egg and sprinkle with remaining cheese. Bake 20 to 25 minutes or until golden and crisp; turn off oven. Pierce each puff with a knife and return to cooling oven for 10 minutes to dry out. Remove and cool.

Drain approximately ¼ cup of liquid from salsa (reserve liquid for another use). Mix drained salsa with cream cheese and spoon filling into puffs.   ***Makes 36 appetizers***

Parties & Cocktails

Party Mix

3 cups bite-size rice cereal
2 cups O-shaped oat cereal
2 cups bite-size shredded wheat cereal
1 cup peanuts or pistachios
1 cup thin pretzel sticks
½ cup butter, melted
1 tablespoon Worcestershire sauce
1 teaspoon seasoned salt
½ teaspoon garlic powder
⅛ teaspoon ground red pepper (optional)

1. Preheat oven to 300°F.

2. Combine cereals, nuts and pretzels in 13×9-inch baking pan.

3. Combine melted butter, Worcestershire sauce, seasoned salt, garlic powder and red pepper in small bowl. Drizzle over cereal mixture; toss lightly to coat.

4. Bake 20 minutes, stirring after 10 minutes; cool. Store in airtight container.

Makes 10 cups

Artichoke and Crabmeat Party Dip

1 container (16 ounces) sour cream (2 cups)
1 packet (1 ounce) HIDDEN VALLEY® The Original Ranch®
   Dips Mix
1 can (14 ounces) artichoke hearts, rinsed, drained and chopped
¾ cup cooked crabmeat, rinsed and drained
2 tablespoons chopped red or green bell pepper
   French bread slices, crackers or fresh vegetables, for dipping

Combine sour cream and dips mix. Stir in artichoke hearts, crabmeat and bell peppers. Chill 30 minutes. Serve with French bread, crackers or fresh vegetables.

Makes 3½ cups

Party Mix

Quick Pimiento Cheese Snacks

2 ounces cream cheese, softened
½ cup (2 ounces) shredded Cheddar cheese
1 jar (2 ounces) diced pimiento, drained
2 tablespoons finely chopped pecans
½ teaspoon hot pepper sauce
24 French bread slices, about ¼ inch thick, or party bread slices

1. Preheat broiler.

2. Combine cream cheese and Cheddar cheese in small bowl; mix well.
Stir in pimiento, pecans and hot pepper sauce.

3. Place bread slices on broiler pan or nonstick baking sheet. Broil,
4 inches from heat, 1 to 2 minutes or until lightly toasted on both sides.

4. Spread cheese mixture evenly onto bread slices. Broil 1 to 2 minutes
or until cheese mixture is hot and bubbly. Transfer to serving plate;
garnish, if desired. *Makes 24 servings*

Garlic & Herb Dip

1 cup sour cream
¼ cup mayonnaise
2 tablespoons chopped green onion
1 teaspoon dried basil leaves
½ teaspoon dried tarragon leaves
1 clove garlic, minced
¼ teaspoon salt
¼ teaspoon black pepper
Assorted fresh vegetable dippers or pita chips

1. Combine all ingredients except dippers in medium bowl until blended.

2. Cover; refrigerate several hours or overnight. Serve with dippers.
Makes about 1¼ cups

Quick Pimiento Cheese Snacks

Savory Seafood Spread

2 packages (8 ounces each) light cream cheese, softened
1 package (8 ounces) imitation crab meat, flaked
2 tablespoons minced green onion
1 tablespoon prepared horseradish
1 tablespoon *Frank's® RedHot®* Original Cayenne Pepper Sauce
1 teaspoon *French's®* Worcestershire Sauce
½ cup sliced almonds
   Paprika
   Crackers
   Vegetable dippers

1. Preheat oven to 375°F. Beat or process cream cheese in electric mixer or food processor until smooth and creamy. Add crab, onion, horseradish, *Frank's RedHot* Sauce and Worcestershire; beat or process until well blended.

2. Spread cream cheese mixture onto 9-inch pie plate. Top with almonds and sprinkle with paprika. Bake 20 minutes or until mixture is heated through and almonds are golden.

3. Serve with crackers or vegetable dippers.   **Makes 3 cups spread**

Prep Time: 10 minutes
Cook Time: 20 minutes

Note   For the basic Martini, shake one part dry vermouth and six parts gin with cracked ice. Strain into martini glasses and serve with olives.

Parties & Cocktails

Savory Seafood Spread

Mini Sausage Quiches

½ cup butter or margarine, softened
3 ounces cream cheese, softened
1 cup all-purpose flour
½ pound **BOB EVANS®** Italian Roll Sausage
1 cup (4 ounces) shredded Swiss cheese
1 tablespoon snipped fresh chives
2 eggs
1 cup half-and-half
¼ teaspoon salt
  Dash cayenne pepper

Beat butter and cream cheese in medium bowl until creamy. Blend in flour; refrigerate 1 hour. Roll into 24 (1-inch) balls; press each into ungreased mini-muffin cup to form pastry shell. Preheat oven to 375°F. To prepare filling, crumble sausage into small skillet. Cook over medium heat until browned, stirring occasionally. Drain off any drippings. Sprinkle evenly into pastry shells in muffin cups; sprinkle with Swiss cheese and chives. Whisk eggs, half-and-half, salt and cayenne until blended; pour into pastry shells. Bake 20 to 30 minutes or until set. Remove from pans. Serve hot. Refrigerate leftovers.

Makes 24 appetizers

Note For a Perfect Manhattan, shake one part sweet vermouth and two parts blended whiskey with cracked ice. Strain into a cocktail glass and serve with a maraschino cherry.

Holiday Shrimp Dip

4½ teaspoons unflavored gelatin
¼ cup cold water
1 can (10¾ ounces) condensed tomato soup
1 (3-ounce) package cream cheese
1 cup mayonnaise
1 (6-ounce) bag frozen small shrimp, thawed
¾ cup finely chopped celery
2 tablespoons grated onion
¼ teaspoon salt
White pepper to taste
Bell peppers for garnish (optional)

1. Dissolve gelatin in cold water in small bowl; set aside. Grease four 1-cup holiday mold pans or one (5½-cup) holiday mold pan; set aside.

2. Heat soup in medium saucepan over medium heat until hot. Add cream cheese; blend well. Add gelatin mixture, mayonnaise, shrimp, celery, onion and seasonings. Pour into prepared mold; refrigerate 30 minutes. Cover with foil and refrigerate overnight.

3. Decorate with bell peppers cut into holly leaves, if desired. Serve with assorted crackers.   ***Makes 12 servings***

Pepper and Parsley Logs

1 packet (1 ounce) HIDDEN VALLEY® The Original Ranch® Salad
    Dressing & Seasoning Mix
8 ounces cream cheese, softened
2 teaspoons cracked pepper
2 teaspoons chopped fresh parsley

Combine salad dressing & seasoning mix and cream cheese. Divide in half; chill until firm. Roll into two 1½-inch logs, coating one with pepper and the other with parsley. Wrap in plastic wrap; chill.   ***Makes 2 logs***

Serving Suggestion: Spread on crackers or bread.

Savory Stuffed Mushrooms

20 medium mushrooms
2 tablespoons finely chopped onion
2 tablespoons finely chopped red bell pepper
3 tablespoons FLEISCHMANN'S® Original Margarine
½ cup dry seasoned bread crumbs
½ teaspoon dried basil leaves

1. Remove stems from mushrooms; finely chop ¼ cup stems.

2. Cook and stir chopped stems, onion and pepper in margarine in skillet over medium heat until tender. Remove from heat; stir in crumbs and basil.

3. Spoon crumb mixture loosely into mushroom caps; place on baking sheet. Bake at 400°F for 15 minutes or until hot.   *Makes 20 appetizers*

Prep Time: 20 minutes
Cook Time: 15 minutes
Total Time: 35 minutes

Salmon Appetizers

1 package frozen puff pastry sheets, thawed
4 ounces smoked salmon, flaked
8 ounces cream cheese, softened
2 tablespoons snipped chives
1½ teaspoons lemon juice

Preheat oven to 375°F. Cut twelve 2-inch rounds of dough from pastry sheet; place in greased muffin cups. (Freeze remaining pastry sheet for later use.) Top dough rounds with salmon. Mix cream cheese, chives and lemon juice until creamy. Top salmon with about 1 tablespoon cream cheese mixture or pipe cream cheese over salmon, if desired. Bake 15 to 18 minutes. Serve warm.   *Makes 12 appetizers*

*Favorite recipe from **Wisconsin Milk Marketing Board***

Savory Stuffed Mushrooms

Smoked Salmon Appetizers

¼ cup cream cheese, softened
1 tablespoon chopped fresh dill *or* 1 teaspoon dried dill weed
⅛ teaspoon ground red pepper
4 ounces thinly sliced smoked salmon or lox
24 melba toast rounds or other crackers

1. Combine cream cheese, dill and pepper in small bowl; stir to blend. Spread evenly over each slice of salmon. Roll up salmon slices jelly-roll fashion. Place on plate; cover with plastic wrap. Chill at least 1 hour or up to 4 hours before serving.

2. Using a sharp knife, cut salmon rolls crosswise into ¾-inch pieces. Place pieces, cut side down, on melba rounds. Garnish each salmon roll with dill sprig, if desired. Serve cold or at room temperature.

Makes about 2 dozen appetizers

Rock Shrimp Mini Quiches

½ pound cooked Florida rock shrimp
1 package (8 ounces) refrigerated butterflake rolls *or* 24 mini pastry shells
1 egg, beaten
½ cup evaporated milk
1 tablespoon cooking sherry
½ teaspoon salt
⅛ teaspoon white pepper
¼ cup grated Parmesan cheese

Finely chop shrimp. Grease cups of two miniature muffin pans. Divide rolls into 24 equal pieces and press each piece into muffin cup to form a shell. Place 1 teaspoon chopped shrimp in each muffin cup.

Combine egg, milk, sherry, salt and pepper. Divide mixture evenly among muffin cups. Top with ½ teaspoon Parmesan cheese. Bake at 375°F 25 minutes.

Makes 24 appetizers

*Favorite recipe from **Florida Department of Agriculture and Consumer Services, Bureau of Seafood and Aquaculture***

Parties & Cocktails

Smoked Salmon Appetizers

Pepper Cheese Cocktail Puffs

½ **package (17¼ ounces) frozen puff pastry, thawed**
1 **tablespoon Dijon mustard**
½ **cup (2 ounces) finely shredded Cheddar cheese**
1 **teaspoon cracked black pepper**
1 **egg**
1 **tablespoon water**

1. Preheat oven to 400°F. Grease baking sheets.

2. Roll out 1 sheet puff pastry dough on well floured surface to 14×10-inch rectangle. Spread half of dough (from 10-inch side) with mustard. Sprinkle with cheese and pepper. Fold dough over filling; roll gently to seal edges.

3. Cut lengthwise into 3 strips; cut each strip diagonally into 1½-inch pieces. Place on prepared baking sheets. Beat egg and water in small bowl; brush on appetizers.

4. Bake appetizers 12 to 15 minutes or until puffed and deep golden brown. Remove from baking sheet to wire rack to cool.

Makes about 20 appetizers

Tip: *Work quickly and efficiently when using puff pastry. The colder puff pastry is, the better it will puff in the hot oven. Also, this recipe can be easily doubled.*

Prep and Bake Time: 30 minutes

Note

To make an Old-Fashioned, combine 2 teaspoons superfine sugar, 2 dashes bitters and 1 teaspoon water in an old-fashioned glass. Stir well. Add ice cubes and 2 ounces blended whiskey. Serve with a slice of orange, a lemon twist and a maraschino cherry.

Pepper Cheese Cocktail Puffs

Wisconsin Asiago Cheese Puffs

1 tablespoon butter
1 tablespoon olive oil
½ teaspoon salt
  Cayenne pepper to taste
1 cup water
1 cup flour
4 eggs*
½ cup (2 ounces) finely shredded Wisconsin Asiago cheese
½ cup (2 ounces) grated Wisconsin Parmesan cheese

For lighter puffs, use 2 whole eggs and 4 egg whites.

Preheat oven to 400°F. In small saucepan, combine butter, oil, salt, cayenne and water; bring to a boil. Add flour all at once; stir until mixture forms a smooth ball. Cook over low heat until mixture is drier but still smooth. Put mixture into mixing bowl; beat in eggs, one at a time. Stir in cheeses. Drop spoonfuls of batter onto greased cookie sheet. Bake for 20 minutes or until slightly browned and firm. Serve immediately.

Makes 30 puffs

*Favorite recipe from **Wisconsin Milk Marketing Board***

Original Ranch® Snack Mix

8 cups KELLOGG'S® CRISPIX®* cereal
2½ cups small pretzels
2½ cups bite-size Cheddar cheese crackers (optional)
3 tablespoons vegetable oil
1 packet (1 ounce) HIDDEN VALLEY® The Original Ranch® Salad Dressing & Seasoning Mix

Kellogg's® and Crispix® are registered trademarks of Kellogg Company.

Combine cereal, pretzels and crackers in a gallon-size Glad® Zipper Storage Bag. Pour oil over mixture. Seal bag and toss to coat. Add salad dressing & seasoning mix; seal bag and toss again until coated.

Makes 10 cups

Parties & Cocktails

Shrimp Spread

½ **pound medium shrimp, peeled and deveined, reserving shells**
1 **cup water**
½ **teaspoon onion powder**
½ **teaspoon garlic salt**
1 **package (8 ounces) cream cheese, softened**
4 **tablespoons butter, softened**
2 **tablespoons mayonnaise**
2 **tablespoons cocktail sauce**
1 **tablespoon lemon juice**
1 **tablespoon chopped fresh parsley**
   Assorted crackers or raw vegetables
   Green onion, star fruit, kiwifruit and radish slices for garnish

Place reserved shrimp shells, water, onion powder and garlic salt in medium saucepan. Bring to a simmer over medium heat; simmer 5 minutes. Remove shells and discard. Add shrimp; simmer 1 minute or until shrimp turn pink and opaque. Remove shrimp and place on cutting board; let cool. Continue cooking shrimp liquid to reduce until it just barely covers bottom of pan.

Blend cream cheese, butter, mayonnaise, cocktail sauce and lemon juice in large bowl until smooth. Stir in 1 tablespoon reduced cooking liquid. Discard remaining liquid.

Chop shrimp finely. Fold shrimp and parsley into cheese mixture.

Pack shrimp spread into decorative serving crock or plastic mold lined with plastic wrap. Cover and refrigerate overnight. Serve shrimp spread in decorative crock or invert mold onto serving platter and remove plastic wrap. Serve with assorted crackers. Garnish, if desired.

Makes 2½ to 3 cups

Popular Proteins

Big roasts, huge steaks, stuffed pork chops, roast chicken and meatballs that graced many '50s dinner tables also remain popular today.

Swanson® Savory Pot Roast with Harvest Vegetables

Swanson® Savory Pot Roast with Harvest Vegetables

2 tablespoons vegetable oil
3 pounds boneless beef bottom round *or* rump roast
1 can (14 ounces) SWANSON® Seasoned Beef Broth with Onion *or* SWANSON® Beef Broth
¾ cup V8® 100% Vegetable Juice
2 cups fresh *or* frozen baby carrots
3 medium potatoes, quartered
3 stalks celery, cut into 1-inch pieces
2 tablespoons all-purpose flour
¼ cup water

HEAT oil in Dutch oven. Add roast and cook until browned on all sides. Pour off fat.

ADD broth and vegetable juice. Heat to a boil. Cover and cook over low heat 1 hour and 45 minutes.

ADD vegetables. Cover and cook 30 minutes or until vegetables are tender. Remove roast and vegetables and keep warm.

MIX flour and water. Add to Dutch oven. Cook and stir until mixture boils and thickens. Serve with roast and vegetables.

Makes 6 servings

Prep Time: 15 minutes
Cook Time: 2 hours 30 minutes

Popular Proteins

Beef Stroganoff

· · · · ● ●

8 ounces uncooked egg noodles
¼ cup all-purpose flour
½ teaspoon salt
¼ teaspoon black pepper
1¼ pounds beef tenderloin steaks or tenderloin tips
¼ cup butter, divided
¾ cup chopped onion
12 ounces fresh button mushrooms, sliced
1 can (10½ ounces) condensed beef broth
2 tablespoons tomato paste
1 tablespoon Worcestershire sauce
1 cup sour cream, at room temperature
Fresh chives for garnish

1. Cook noodles according to package directions; drain and keep warm.

2. Meanwhile, combine flour, salt and pepper in large resealable plastic food storage bag. Cut beef into 1½×½-inch strips; add ½ of beef to flour mixture. Seal bag; shake to coat well. Repeat with remaining beef. Discard remaining flour.

3. Melt 1 tablespoon butter in large nonstick skillet over medium-high heat. Add ½ of beef mixture to skillet. Cook and stir until browned on all sides. *Do not overcook.* Transfer to medium bowl. Repeat with 1 tablespoon butter and remaining beef mixture; transfer to same bowl. Set aside.

4. Melt remaining 2 tablespoons butter in same skillet over medium-high heat. Add onion; cook 5 minutes, stirring occasionally. Add mushrooms; cook and stir 5 minutes or until mushrooms are tender.

5. Stir in broth, tomato paste and Worcestershire sauce; bring to a boil, scraping up any browned bits.

6. Return beef mixture and any accumulated juices to skillet; cook about 5 minutes or until heated through and sauce thickens. Stir in sour cream; heat through. *Do not boil.*

7. Serve beef mixture over reserved noodles. Garnish, if desired.

Makes 4 servings

Beef Stroganoff

Swanson® Rosemary Chicken & Vegetables

3- to 4-pound whole broiler-fryer chicken
1 tablespoon butter *or* margarine, melted
4 medium red potatoes, quartered
2 cups fresh *or* frozen baby carrots
2 stalks celery, cut into chunks
12 small white onions, peeled
1½ teaspoon chopped fresh rosemary *or* ½ teaspoon dried
    rosemary leaves, crushed
1 cup SWANSON® Chicken Broth
½ cup orange juice

BRUSH chicken with butter. Place chicken and vegetables in roasting pan. Sprinkle with rosemary. Mix broth and orange juice and pour **half** of broth mixture over all.

ROAST at 375°F. for 1 hour.

STIR vegetables. Add remaining broth mixture to pan. Roast 30 minutes or until done.   *Makes 4 servings*

Prep Time: 15 minutes
Cook Time: 1 hour 30 minutes

Tip To quickly peel onions, pour boiling water over onions and let stand 5 minutes. Then slip off skins.

Swanson® Rosemary Chicken & Vegetables

Swedish-Style Meatballs

4 tablespoons butter or margarine, divided
1 cup minced onions
1 pound 90% lean ground beef
½ pound lean ground veal
½ pound lean ground pork
1 cup fresh bread crumbs
2 eggs, lightly beaten
½ teaspoon salt
¼ teaspoon black pepper
⅛ teaspoon grated nutmeg
3 tablespoons all-purpose flour
1¼ cups milk
¼ cup half-and-half
1 egg yolk
½ teaspoon salt

Melt 2 tablespoons butter in large skillet over medium heat. Add onions. Cook and stir 8 to 10 minutes or until onions are very soft. Remove from heat and set aside. Combine beef, veal, pork, bread crumbs, beaten eggs, salt, pepper and nutmeg in large bowl. Add onions; mix well. Shape into balls (use 2 tablespoons of meat mixture for dinner-size meatball). Set aside.

Preheat oven to 200°F.

Reheat skillet over medium heat. Add ¼ to ⅓ of meatballs. *Do not crowd pan.* Cook 8 minutes, shaking pan to allow meatballs to roll and brown evenly. Reduce heat to medium-low. Cook 15 to 20 minutes or until cooked through. Transfer to covered casserole dish and keep warm in oven. Repeat until all meatballs are cooked.

Meanwhile, wipe out skillet. Melt remaining 2 tablespoons butter over medium heat. Whisk in flour. Stir well. Combine milk, half-and-half, egg yolk and salt in small bowl. Slowly stir into flour mixture. Reduce heat to medium-low. Cook and stir 3 minutes or until thickened. Remove dish from oven and pour sauce over meatballs. Serve immediately.

Makes 36 dinner-size meatballs

Popular Proteins

Swedish-Style Meatballs

Herb-Crusted Roast Beef and Potatoes

1 (4½-pound) eye of round or sirloin tip beef roast
¾ cup plus 2 tablespoons FILIPPO BERIO® Olive Oil, divided
   Salt and freshly ground black pepper
2 tablespoons paprika
2 pounds small red skin potatoes, cut into halves
1 cup dry bread crumbs
1 teaspoon dried thyme leaves
1 teaspoon dried rosemary
½ teaspoon salt
¼ teaspoon freshly ground black pepper

Preheat oven to 325°F. Brush roast with 2 tablespoons olive oil. Season to taste with salt and pepper. Place in large roasting pan; insert meat thermometer into center of thickest part of roast. Roast 45 minutes.

Meanwhile, in large bowl, combine ½ cup olive oil and paprika. Add potatoes; toss until lightly coated. In small bowl, combine bread crumbs, thyme, rosemary, ½ teaspoon salt, ¼ teaspoon pepper and remaining ¼ cup olive oil.

Carefully remove roast from oven. Place potatoes around roast. Press bread crumb mixture onto top of roast to form crust. Sprinkle any remaining bread crumb mixture over potatoes. Roast an additional 40 to 45 minutes or until meat thermometer registers 145°F for medium-rare or until desired doneness is reached. Transfer roast to carving board; tent with foil. Let stand 5 to 10 minutes before carving. Cut into ¼-inch-thick slices. Serve immediately with potatoes, spooning any bread crumb mixture from roasting pan onto meat. *Makes 8 servings*

Herb-Crusted Roast Beef and Potatoes

Cheesy Pork Chops 'n' Potatoes

1 jar (8 ounces) pasteurized processed cheese spread
1 tablespoon vegetable oil
6 thin pork chops, ¼ to ½ inch thick
  Seasoned salt
½ cup milk
4 cups frozen cottage fries
1⅓ cups *French's®* French Fried Onions, divided
1 package (10 ounces) frozen broccoli spears,* thawed and
  drained

*1 small head fresh broccoli (about ½ pound) can be substituted for frozen spears. Divide
into spears and cook 3 to 4 minutes before using.*

Preheat oven to 350°F. Spoon cheese spread into 12×8-inch baking dish;
place in oven just until cheese melts, about 5 minutes. Meanwhile, in
large skillet, heat oil. Brown pork chops on both sides; drain. Sprinkle
chops with seasoned salt; set aside. Using fork, stir milk into melted
cheese until well blended. Stir cottage fries and *⅔ cup* French Fried
Onions into cheese mixture. Divide broccoli spears into 6 small bunches.
Arrange bunches of spears over potato mixture with flowerets around
edges of dish. Arrange chops over broccoli *stalks*. Bake, covered, at
350°F for 35 to 40 minutes or until pork chops are no longer pink. Top
chops with remaining *⅔ cup* onions; bake, uncovered, 5 minutes or until
onions are golden brown.   **Makes 4 to 6 servings**

Popular Proteins

Side by Side Southern Stuffing and Turkey

1 (3-pound) BUTTERBALL® Boneless Breast of Young Turkey
with Gravy Packet, thawed
Vegetable oil
1 can (14½ ounces) chicken broth
½ cup chopped onion
½ cup chopped celery
4 tablespoons butter or margarine
4 cups packaged cornbread stuffing
1 can (16 ounces) sliced peaches, drained and coarsely chopped
½ cup chopped pecans

Spray small roasting pan with nonstick cooking spray. Place boneless breast on one side of roasting pan. Brush with vegetable oil. Combine chicken broth, onion, celery and butter in large saucepan; simmer 5 minutes over low heat. Add stuffing, peaches and pecans; lightly toss mixture. Place stuffing alongside boneless breast. Cover stuffing with foil. Bake in preheated 325°F oven 1 hour and 45 minutes or until internal temperature reaches 170°F. Let boneless breast stand 10 minutes for easy carving. Prepare gravy according to package directions. Serve turkey with gravy and stuffing.   *Makes 6 servings*

Prep Time: 15 minutes plus roasting time

The best way to determine doneness of meats and poultry is to use a thermometer to check the temperature. The temperature can be measured with an instant read thermometer that is inserted just before a reading is taken and is then removed.

Beef in Wine Sauce

4 pounds boneless beef chuck roast, cut into 1½- to 2-inch cubes
2 tablespoons garlic powder
2 cans (10¾ ounces each) condensed golden mushroom soup, undiluted
1 can (8 ounces) sliced mushrooms, drained
¾ cup dry sherry
1 envelope (about 1 ounce) dry onion soup mix
1 bag (20 ounces) frozen sliced carrots

1. Preheat oven to 325°F. Spray heavy 4-quart casserole or Dutch oven with nonstick cooking spray.

2. Sprinkle beef with garlic powder. Place in prepared casserole.

3. Combine canned soup, mushrooms, sherry and dry soup mix in medium bowl. Pour over meat; mix well.

4. Cover and bake 3 hours or until meat is very tender. Add carrots during last 15 minutes of baking.   ***Makes 6 to 8 servings***

Tip If you don't have time to cube a boneless beef chuck roast, purchase beef for stew which is already cubed. Brown the beef cubes in a small amount of oil in batches to add extra flavor to the beef.

Beef in Wine Sauce

Browned Pork Chops with Gravy

4 boneless pork loin chops (12 ounces)
½ teaspoon dried sage leaves
½ teaspoon dried marjoram leaves
¼ teaspoon black pepper
⅛ teaspoon salt
   Nonstick olive oil cooking spray
¼ cup coarsely chopped onion
1 clove garlic, minced
1 cup sliced mushrooms
¾ cup beef broth
⅓ cup sour cream
1 tablespoon all-purpose flour
1 teaspoon Dijon mustard
2 cups hot cooked noodles
   Snipped parsley (optional)

1. Trim fat from chops. Stir together sage, marjoram, pepper and salt. Rub on both sides of chops. Spray large nonstick skillet with cooking spray; heat over medium heat. Place chops in skillet. Cook 5 minutes, turning once, or until chops are just barely pink. Remove chops from skillet; keep warm.

2. Add onion and garlic to skillet; cook and stir 2 minutes. Add mushrooms and broth. Bring to a boil. Reduce heat and simmer, covered, 3 to 4 minutes or until mushrooms are tender.

3. Whisk together sour cream, flour and mustard in medium bowl. Whisk in about 3 tablespoons broth from skillet. Stir sour cream mixture into skillet. Cook, stirring constantly, until mixture comes to a boil. Serve over pork chops and noodles. Sprinkle with parsley, if desired.

Makes 4 servings

Popular Proteins

Browned Pork Chop with Gravy

Mustard Crusted Rib Roast

1 (3-rib) beef rib roast, trimmed* (6 to 7 pounds)
3 tablespoons Dijon mustard
1 tablespoon plus 1½ teaspoons chopped fresh tarragon
    or 1½ teaspoons dried tarragon leaves
3 cloves garlic, minced
¼ cup dry red wine
⅓ cup finely chopped shallots (about 2 shallots)
1 tablespoon all-purpose flour
1 cup beef broth
    Mashed potatoes
    Fresh tarragon sprigs for garnish

Ask meat retailer to remove chine bone for easier carving. Trim fat to ¼-inch thickness.

1. Preheat oven to 450°F. Place roast, bone-side-down, in shallow roasting pan. Combine mustard, chopped tarragon and garlic in small bowl; spread over all surfaces of roast, except bottom. Insert meat thermometer into thickest part of roast, not touching bone or fat. Roast 10 minutes.

2. Reduce oven temperature to 350°F. Roast 2½ to 3 hours for medium or until internal temperature reaches 145°F when tested with meat thermometer inserted into thickest part of roast, without touching bone.

3. Transfer roast to cutting board; cover with foil. Let stand 10 to 15 minutes before carving. Internal temperature will continue to rise 5°F to 10°F during stand time.

4. To make gravy, pour fat from roasting pan, reserving 1 tablespoon in medium saucepan. Add wine to roasting pan; place over 2 burners. Cook over medium heat 2 minutes or until slightly thickened, stirring to scrape up browned bits; reserve.

5. Add shallots to reserved drippings in saucepan; cook and stir over medium heat 4 minutes or until softened. Add flour; cook and stir 1 minute. Add broth and reserved wine mixture; cook 5 minutes or until sauce thickens, stirring occasionally. Pour through strainer into gravy boat, pressing with back of spoon on shallots; discard solids.

6. Carve roast into ½-inch-thick slices. Serve with mashed potatoes and gravy. Garnish, if desired. **Makes 6 to 8 servings**

Mustard Crusted Rib Roast

Lemon Rosemary Roast Chicken

····●●●

1 whole chicken (about 4 to 4½ pounds)
2½ teaspoons LAWRY'S® Seasoned Salt
2 teaspoons whole dried rosemary, crumbled
1 teaspoon LAWRY'S® Lemon Pepper

Rinse chicken with cold water; pat dry with paper towels. In small bowl, combine Seasoned Salt, rosemary and Lemon Pepper. Gently lift skin from meat on breast. Rub seasoning mixture onto meat under skin, all over outside of chicken and inside cavity. Spray 13×9×2-inch baking dish with nonstick cooking spray; add chicken, breast-side-up. Roast in 400°F oven until meat is no longer pink and juices run clear when cut (175°-180°F at thickest joint), about 60 to 70 minutes. Let stand 10 minutes before carving. **Makes 8 servings**

Hint: Loosely 'crunch up' some foil in dish around chicken to keep grease from splattering in oven. Also, elevate chicken on cooling rack in dish to help brown bottom of chicken.

Steaks with Mushroom Onion Sauce

····●●●

1½ pounds boneless beef sirloin steak
2 cups sliced fresh mushrooms
1 medium onion, thinly sliced
1 jar (12 ounces) HEINZ® Fat Free Savory Beef Gravy
1 tablespoon HEINZ® Tomato Ketchup
1 teaspoon HEINZ® Worcestershire Sauce
Dash pepper

Cut steak into 6 portions. Spray a large skillet with nonstick cooking spray. Cook steak over medium high heat to desired doneness, about 5 minutes per side for medium-rare. Remove and keep warm. In same skillet, cook mushrooms and onion until liquid evaporates. Stir in gravy, ketchup, Worcestershire sauce and pepper; simmer 1 minute, stirring occasionally. Serve sauce over steak.

Makes 6 servings (about 2 cups sauce)

Lemon Rosemary Roast Chicken

Pepper Steak

1 tablespoon coarsely cracked black pepper
½ teaspoon dried rosemary
2 beef tenderloin or ribeye steaks (4 to 6 ounces each)
1 tablespoon butter or margarine
1 tablespoon vegetable oil
  Salt
¼ cup brandy or dry red wine

1. Combine pepper and rosemary in bowl. Coat both sides of steaks with mixture.

2. Heat butter and oil in large skillet until hot; add steaks and cook over medium heat 5 to 7 minutes per side for medium rare to medium or until desired doneness. Remove steaks from skillet. Sprinkle lightly with salt and cover to keep warm.

3. Add brandy to skillet; bring to a boil over high heat, scraping particles from bottom of skillet. Boil about 1 minute or until liquid is reduced by half. Spoon sauce over steaks. ***Makes 2 servings***

Prep and Cook Time: 17 minutes

Note Filet mignon and rib-eye steaks are two of the most tender cuts of meat. These choice cuts are well-suited to quick, dry-heat cooking methods such as pan-frying, broiling and grilling.

Pepper Steak

The Original Baked SPAM®

. . • • ● ●

1 (12-ounce) can SPAM® Classic
   Whole cloves
⅓ cup packed brown sugar
1 teaspoon water
1 teaspoon prepared mustard
½ teaspoon vinegar

Heat oven to 375°F. Place SPAM® on rack in shallow baking pan. Score surface; stud with cloves. In small bowl, combine brown sugar, water, mustard and vinegar, stirring until smooth. Brush glaze over SPAM®. Bake 20 minutes, basting often. Cut into slices to serve.

Makes 6 servings

Hearty Shepherd's Pie

. . • • ● ●

1½ pounds ground beef
2 cups *French's®* French Fried Onions
1 can (10¾ ounces) condensed tomato soup
2 teaspoons Italian seasoning
1 package (10 ounces) frozen mixed vegetables, thawed
3 cups hot mashed potatoes

1. Preheat oven to 375°F. Cook meat in large oven-proof skillet until browned; drain. Stir in *1 cup* French Fried Onions, soup, *½ cup water,* seasoning and *¼ teaspoon each salt and pepper.*

2. Spoon vegetables over beef mixture. Top with mashed potatoes.

3. Bake 20 minutes or until hot. Sprinkle with remaining *1 cup* onions. Bake 2 minutes or until golden.

Makes 6 servings

Prep Time: 10 minutes
Cook Time: 27 minutes

Campbell's® Autumn Pork Chops

1 tablespoon vegetable oil
4 pork chops, ¾ inch thick (about 1½ pounds)
1 can (10¾ ounces) CAMPBELL'S® Condensed Cream of Celery
Soup *or* 98% Fat Free Cream of Celery Soup
½ cup apple juice *or* water
2 tablespoons spicy brown mustard
1 tablespoon honey
Generous dash pepper

1. In medium skillet over medium-high heat, heat oil. Add chops and cook 10 minutes or until browned. Set chops aside. Pour off fat.

2. Add soup, apple juice, mustard, honey and pepper. Heat to a boil. Return chops to pan. Reduce heat to low. Cover and cook 10 minutes or until chops are no longer pink. *Makes 4 servings*

Prep Time: 5 minutes
Cook Time: 25 minutes

Tip You can store uncooked fresh pork tightly wrapped in butcher paper in the refrigerator up to four or five days. Freeze uncooked pork for up to one month.

Popular Proteins

Backyard Barbecue

The popularity of outdoor grilling soared in the '50s. Step into the suburban backyard and enjoy tasty steaks, spicy chicken, juicy burgers and more!

Pork Chop with Apple-Sage Stuffing

Pork Chops with Apple-Sage Stuffing

6 center-cut pork chops (3 pounds), about 1 inch thick
¾ cup dry vermouth, divided
4 tablespoons minced fresh sage *or* 4 teaspoons rubbed sage, divided
2 tablespoons soy sauce
1 tablespoon olive oil
2 cloves garlic, minced
½ teaspoon black pepper, divided
1 tablespoon butter
1 medium onion, diced
1 apple, cored and diced
½ teaspoon salt
2 cups fresh firm-textured white bread crumbs
Curly endive
Plum slices

Cut pocket in each chop using tip of thin, sharp knife. Combine ¼ cup vermouth, 2 tablespoons fresh sage (or 2 teaspoons rubbed sage), soy sauce, oil, garlic and ¼ teaspoon pepper in glass dish; add pork chops, turning to coat. Heat butter in large skillet over medium heat until foamy. Add onion and apple; cook and stir about 6 minutes until onion is tender. Stir in remaining ½ cup vermouth, 2 tablespoons sage, ¼ teaspoon pepper and salt. Cook and stir over high heat about 3 minutes until liquid is almost gone. Transfer onion mixture to large bowl. Stir in bread crumbs.

Remove pork chops from marinade; discard marinade. Spoon onion mixture into pockets of pork chops. Close openings with wooden picks. (Soak wooden picks in hot water 15 minutes to prevent burning.) Grill pork chops on covered grill over medium KINGSFORD® Briquets about 5 minutes per side until barely pink in center. Garnish with endive and plum slices. *Makes 6 servings*

Rosemary Garlic Rub

2 tablespoons chopped fresh rosemary
1½ teaspoons LAWRY'S® Seasoned Salt
1 teaspoon LAWRY'S® Garlic Pepper
½ teaspoon LAWRY'S® Garlic Powder with Parsley
1 pound beef top sirloin steak
1 tablespoon olive oil

In small bowl, combine rosemary, Seasoned Salt, Garlic Pepper and Garlic Powder with Parsley; mix well. Brush both sides of steak with oil. Sprinkle with herb mixture, pressing onto steak. Grill or broil steak 15 to 20 minutes or until desired doneness, turning halfway through grilling time.
Makes 4 servings

Prep Time: 2 minutes
Cook Time: 15 to 20 minutes

Mustard-Glazed Ribs

¾ cup beer
½ cup firmly packed dark brown sugar
½ cup spicy brown mustard
3 tablespoons soy sauce
1 tablespoon catsup
¾ teaspoon TABASCO® brand Pepper Sauce
½ teaspoon ground cloves
4 pounds pork spareribs or baby back ribs

Combine beer, sugar, mustard, soy sauce, catsup, TABASCO® Sauce and cloves in medium bowl; mix well. Position grill rack as far from coals as possible. Place ribs on grill over low heat. For spareribs, grill 45 minutes; turn occasionally. Brush with mustard glaze. Grill 30 minutes longer or until meat is cooked through; turn and baste ribs often with mustard glaze. (For baby back ribs, grill 15 minutes. Brush with mustard glaze. Grill 30 minutes longer or until meat is cooked to desired doneness; turn and baste ribs often with mustard glaze.) Heat any remaining glaze to a boil; serve with ribs.
Makes 4 servings

Rosemary Garlic Rub

Sweet and Spicy Chicken Barbecue

1½ cups DOLE® Pineapple Orange Juice
1 cup orange marmalade
⅔ cup teriyaki sauce
½ cup firmly packed brown sugar
½ teaspoon ground cloves
½ teaspoon ground ginger
4 broiler-fryer chickens, halved or quartered (about 2 pounds each)
Salt and pepper
1 can (20 ounces) DOLE® Pineapple Slices, drained
4 teaspoons cornstarch

• In saucepan, combine juice, marmalade, teriyaki sauce, brown sugar, cloves and ginger. Heat over medium heat until sugar dissolves; let cool. Sprinkle chicken with salt and pepper. Place chicken in glass baking dish. Pour juice mixture over chicken; turn to coat all sides. Marinate, covered, 2 hours in refrigerator, turning often.

• Preheat oven to 350°F. Light charcoal grill. Drain chicken; reserve marinade. Bake chicken 20 minutes. Arrange chicken on lightly greased grill, 4 to 6 inches above glowing coals. Grill, turning and basting often with reserved marinade, 20 to 25 minutes or until meat near bone is no longer pink. Grill pineapple slices 3 minutes or until heated through.

• In small saucepan, dissolve cornstarch in remaining marinade. Cook over medium heat until sauce boils and thickens. Spoon over chicken. Serve chicken with pineapple. **_Makes 8 servings_**

Backyard Barbecue

Sweet and Spicy Chicken Barbecue

The All-American Burger

Burger Spread (recipe follows)
1½ pounds ground beef
2 tablespoons chopped fresh parsley
2 teaspoons onion powder
2 teaspoons Worcestershire sauce
1 teaspoon garlic powder
1 teaspoon salt
1 teaspoon black pepper
4 hamburger buns, split

1. Prepare Burger Spread; set aside.

2. Prepare grill for direct cooking.

3. Combine beef with parsley, onion powder, Worcestershire sauce, garlic powder, salt and pepper in medium bowl; mix lightly, but thoroughly. Shape mixture into four ½-inch-thick burgers.

4. Place burgers on grid. Grill, covered, over medium heat 8 to 10 minutes (or, uncovered, 13 to 15 minutes) to medium doneness (160°F) or to desired doneness, turning halfway through grilling time.

5. Remove burgers from grill. Place burgers between buns; top each burger with Burger Spread. *Makes 4 servings*

Burger Spread

½ cup ketchup
¼ cup prepared mustard
2 tablespoons chopped onion
1 tablespoon relish or chopped pickles
1 tablespoon chopped fresh parsley

Combine all ingredients in small bowl; mix well. *Makes 1 cup*

Backyard Barbecue

Pork Tenderloin with Orange Glaze

The Definitive Steak

4 New York strip steaks (about 5 ounces each)
4 tablespoons olive oil
2 teaspoons minced garlic
1 teaspoon salt
½ teaspoon black pepper

Place steaks in shallow glass container. Combine oil, garlic, salt and pepper in small bowl; mix well. Pour oil mixture over steaks; turn to coat well. Cover; refrigerate 30 to 60 minutes.

Prepare grill for direct cooking.

Place steaks on grid. Grill, covered, over medium-high heat 14 minutes for medium, 20 minutes for well or according to desired doneness, turning halfway through grilling time.   ***Makes 4 servings***

Zesty Onion Burgers

1½ pounds ground beef
1⅓ cups *French's*® French Fried Onions, divided
3 tablespoons *French's*® Bold n' Spicy Brown Mustard
1 tablespoon prepared horseradish
¾ teaspoon garlic salt
¼ teaspoon ground black pepper
** Lettuce leaves**
** Tomato slices**
6 kaiser rolls

Combine beef, *⅔ cup* French Fried Onions, mustard, horseradish, garlic salt and ground pepper in large bowl. Shape into 6 patties.

Place patties on oiled grid. Grill* over medium coals 10 minutes or until no longer pink in center, turning once.

Arrange lettuce, tomatoes and burgers on rolls. Top with remaining *⅔ cup* onions.   ***Makes 6 servings***

Or, broil 6 inches from heat.

Backyard Barbecue

Hot Diggity Dogs

2 tablespoons butter or margarine
2 large (1 pound) sweet onions, thinly sliced
½ cup *French's*® Classic Yellow® Mustard
½ cup ketchup
10 frankfurters
10 frankfurter buns

Melt butter in medium skillet over medium heat. Add onion; cook 10 minutes or until very tender, stirring often. Stir in mustard and ketchup. Cook over low heat 2 minutes, stirring often.

Place frankfurters and buns on grid. Grill over medium coals 5 minutes or until frankfurters are browned and buns are toasted, turning once. To serve, spoon onion mixture into buns; top each with 1 frankfurter.

Makes 10 servings (about 2½ cups onion topping)

Prep Time: 5 minutes
Cook Time: 20 minutes

Tip Onion topping is also great on hamburgers or smoked sausage heros.

Backyard Barbecue

Hawaiian-Style Burgers

1½ **pounds ground beef**
⅓ **cup chopped green onions**
2 **tablespoons Worcestershire sauce**
⅛ **teaspoon black pepper**
⅓ **cup pineapple preserves**
⅓ **cup barbecue sauce**
6 **pineapple slices**
6 **hamburger buns, split and toasted**

1. Combine beef, onions, Worcestershire and pepper in large bowl. Shape into six 1-inch-thick patties.

2. Combine preserves and barbecue sauce in small saucepan. Bring to a boil over medium heat, stirring often.

3. Place patties on grill rack directly above medium coals. Grill, covered, 8 to 10 minutes (or, uncovered, 13 to 15 minutes) to medium doneness (160°F), turning and brushing often with sauce. Place pineapple on grill; grill 1 minute or until browned, turning once.

4. To serve, place patties on buns with pineapple. **Makes 6 servings**

Broiling Directions: Arrange patties on rack in broiler pan. Broil 4 inches from heat to medium doneness (160°F), turning and brushing often with sauce. Broil pineapple 1 minute, turning once.

Backyard Barbecue

Hot and Spicy Spareribs

1 rack pork spareribs (3 pounds)
2 tablespoons butter or margarine
1 medium onion, finely chopped
2 cloves garlic, minced
1 can (15 ounces) tomato sauce
⅔ cup packed brown sugar
⅔ cup cider vinegar
2 tablespoons chili powder
1 tablespoon prepared mustard
½ teaspoon black pepper

Melt butter in large skillet over low heat. Add onion and garlic; cook and stir until tender. Add remaining ingredients, except ribs, and bring to a boil. Reduce heat and simmer 20 minutes, stirring occasionally.

Place large piece of aluminum foil over coals to catch drippings. Baste meaty side of ribs with sauce. Place ribs on grill, meaty side down, about 6 inches above low coals; baste top side. Cover. Cook about 20 minutes; turn ribs and baste. Cook 45 minutes more or until done, basting every 10 to 15 minutes with sauce.   *Makes 3 servings*

*Favorite recipe from **National Pork Board***

Tip

To reduce grilling time, place 2 pounds of ribs in a single layer in a microwavable glass dish. Add ¼ cup of water and cover with plastic wrap. Heat at MEDIUM (50% power) about 7½ minutes, turning pieces over halfway through cooking time. Drain ribs and proceed with your favorite grilling recipe, reducing the grilling time to about 20 minutes or until done.

Backyard Barbecue

Hot and Spicy Spareribs

Peppercorn Steaks

2 tablespoons olive oil
1 to 2 teaspoons cracked red or black peppercorns or freshly
   ground pepper
1 teaspoon minced garlic
1 teaspoon dried herbs, such as rosemary or parsley
4 boneless beef top loin (strip) or ribeye steaks
   Salt

1. Combine oil, peppercorns, garlic and herbs in small bowl. Rub mixture on both sides of each steak. Cover and refrigerate.

2. Prepare grill for direct cooking.

3. Place steaks on grid over medium heat. Grill, uncovered, 10 to 12 minutes for medium rare to medium or to desired doneness, turning occasionally. Season with salt after cooking.   ***Makes 4 servings***

Grilled Tropical Shrimp

¼ cup barbecue sauce
2 tablespoons pineapple juice or orange juice
10 ounces medium shrimp in shells
2 medium firm nectarines
1 yellow onion, cut into 8 wedges, *or* 6 green onions, cut into
   2-inch lengths

1. Stir together barbecue sauce and pineapple juice. Set aside.

2. Peel and devein shrimp. Cut each nectarine into 6 wedges. Thread shrimp, nectarines and onion wedges onto 4 long metal skewers.

3. Spray grill grid with nonstick cooking spray. Prepare grill for direct grilling. Grill skewers over medium coals 4 to 5 minutes or until shrimp are opaque, turning once and brushing frequently with barbecue sauce.
      Makes 2 servings

Peppercorn Steak

Grilled Marinated Chicken

8 whole chicken leg quarters (about 3½ pounds)
6 ounces frozen lemonade concentrate, thawed
2 tablespoons white wine vinegar
1 tablespoon grated lemon peel
2 cloves garlic, minced

1. Remove skin and all visible fat from chicken. Place chicken in 13×9-inch glass baking dish. Combine remaining ingredients in small bowl; blend well. Pour over chicken; turn to coat. Cover; refrigerate 3 hours or overnight, turning occasionally.

2. To prevent sticking, spray grid with nonstick cooking spray. Prepare coals for grilling.

3. Place chicken on grill 4 inches from medium-hot coals. Grill 20 to 30 minutes or until chicken is no longer pink near bone, turning occasionally. (Do not overcook or chicken will be dry.) Garnish with curly endive and lemon peel strips, if desired. *Makes 8 servings*

Cider Glazed Pork Roast

1 pork loin roast (4 to 5 pounds), boned and tied
½ cup apple cider
¼ cup Dijon-style mustard
¼ cup vegetable oil
¼ cup soy sauce

Insert meat thermometer in center of thickest part of roast. Arrange medium-hot KINGSFORD® Briquets around drip pan. Place roast over drip pan. Cover grill and cook 2½ to 3 hours, or until thermometer registers 160°F, adding more briquets as necessary. Combine apple cider, mustard, oil and soy sauce. Brush roast with cider mixture 3 or 4 times during last 30 minutes of cooking. *Makes 6 servings*

Grilled Marinated Chicken

Beef with Dry Spice Rub

      3 tablespoons firmly packed brown sugar
      1 tablespoon yellow mustard seeds
      1 tablespoon whole coriander seeds
      1 tablespoon black peppercorns
      4 cloves garlic
   1½ to 2 pounds beef top round (London Broil) steak, about
         1½ inches thick
      Vegetable or olive oil
      Salt

Place sugar, mustard seeds, coriander seeds, peppercorns and garlic in blender or food processor; process until seeds and garlic are crushed. Rub beef with oil; pat on spice mixture. Season generously with salt.

Lightly oil hot grid to prevent sticking. Grill beef, on covered grill, over medium-low KINGSFORD® Briquets 16 to 20 minutes for medium rare or until desired doneness, turning once. Let stand 5 minutes before cutting across the grain into thin diagonal slices.   *Makes 6 servings*

Grilled Honey Garlic Pork Chops

      ¼ cup lemon juice
      ¼ cup honey
      2 tablespoons soy sauce
      1 tablespoon dry sherry
      2 cloves garlic, minced
      4 boneless center-cut lean pork chops (about 4 ounces each)

Combine all ingredients except pork chops in small bowl. Place pork in shallow baking dish; pour marinade over pork. Cover and refrigerate 4 hours or overnight. Remove pork from marinade. Heat remaining marinade in small saucepan over medium heat to a simmer. Grill pork over medium-hot coals 12 to 15 minutes, turning once during cooking and basting frequently with marinade, until meat thermometer registers 155° to 160°F.   *Makes 4 servings*

*Favorite recipe from **National Honey Board***

Backyard Barbecue

Beef with Dry Spice Rub

Honey-Garlic Pork Chops

4 boneless center pork loin chops, 1¼- to 1½-inch thickness
¼ cup lemon juice
¼ cup honey
2 tablespoons soy sauce
1 tablespoon dry sherry
2 cloves garlic, minced

Combine all ingredients except chops. Pour over chops in resealable plastic food storage bag; seal. Refrigerate 4 to 24 hours. Prepare covered grill with drip pan in center banked by medium-hot coals. Remove chops from marinade, reserve marinade. Grill chops 12 to 15 minutes, turning once, and basting occasionally with reserved marinade. To broil, place chops 5 inches from heat source, turning once, 12 to 15 minutes or until barely pink in center.   *Makes 4 servings*

Favorite recipe from **National Pork Board**

Sizzle Marinated Steak

2 pounds boneless sirloin or top round steak
½ cup *French's*® Worcestershire Sauce
½ cup red wine vinegar
¼ cup *French's*® Napa Valley Style Dijon Mustard
¼ cup olive oil
1 teaspoon minced garlic

1. Place steak into deep dish or resealable plastic food storage bag.

2. Combine remaining ingredients in small bowl. Pour over steak. Marinate in refrigerator 30 minutes. Broil or grill about 5 minutes per side or until desired doneness. Serve with Signature Steak Sauce.
           Makes 8 servings

Signature Steak Sauce: Combine ½ cup ketchup, ¼ cup **French's**® *Worcestershire Sauce, 1 tablespoon* **Frank's**® **RedHot**® *Sauce and 1 teaspoon minced garlic in small bowl until well blended.*

Backyard Barbecue

Honey-Garlic Pork Chop

Sweet 'n' Smoky BBQ Sauce

½ cup ketchup
⅓ cup *French's®* Bold n' Spicy Brown Mustard
⅓ cup light molasses
¼ cup *French's®* Worcestershire Sauce
¼ teaspoon liquid smoke or hickory salt (optional)

Combine ketchup, mustard, molasses, Worcestershire and liquid smoke, if desired, in medium bowl. Mix until well blended. Brush on chicken or ribs during last 15 minutes of grilling.   *Makes about 1½ cups sauce*

Prep Time: 5 minutes

Orchard BBQ Sauce

2 cloves garlic, minced
1 (24-ounce) jar MOTT'S® Apple Sauce
½ cup apple-cider vinegar
½ cup tomato paste
¼ cup GRANDMA'S® Molasses
¼ cup soy sauce
1 teaspoon paprika
¼ to ½ teaspoon ground red pepper

1. Spray medium nonstick saucepan with nonstick cooking spray; heat over medium heat until hot. Add garlic. Cook and stir 2 to 3 minutes; do not brown.

2. Add apple sauce, vinegar, tomato paste, molasses, soy sauce, paprika and ground red pepper; stir until blended. Increase heat to high; bring mixture to a boil. Cover; reduce heat to low. Simmer 10 minutes, stirring occasionally.

3. Store up to 2 weeks in tightly sealed container in refrigerator.

Makes 16 servings

Sweet 'n' Smoky BBQ Sauce

Way-Out Western BBQ Sauce

½ cup chili sauce
¼ cup fresh lemon juice
¼ cup ketchup
2 tablespoons dry mustard
2 tablespoons brown sugar
2 tablespoons cider vinegar
2 tablespoons dark molasses
1 tablespoon Worcestershire sauce
2 teaspoons grated fresh lemon peel
½ teaspoon garlic powder
½ teaspoon ground allspice
½ teaspoon liquid smoke (optional)
¼ teaspoon hot pepper sauce

Place all ingredients in small bowl and stir until blended. Brush on meats during last 15 minutes of grilling or at beginning of grilling if cooking time is less than 15 minutes.

Makes 10 servings

Tip

Because it has such a high sugar content, barbecue sauce often burns easily. To prevent this, brush sauce on only during the last 15 minutes of grilling or serve it on the side.

Backyard Barbecue

Way-Out Western BBQ Sauce

Kabobs Galore

Charm your family with sensational skewered food—a fun '50s fad. Whether broiled, grilled or no-cook—the possibilities are unlimited.

Hickory Beef Kabob

Hickory Beef Kabobs

1 pound boneless beef top sirloin or tenderloin steaks, cut into
  1¼-inch pieces
2 ears fresh corn,* shucked, cleaned and cut crosswise into
  1-inch pieces
1 red or green bell pepper, cut into 1-inch squares
1 small red onion, cut into ½-inch wedges
½ cup beer
½ cup chili sauce
1 teaspoon dry mustard
2 cloves garlic, minced
3 cups hot cooked white rice
¼ cup chopped fresh parsley

Four small ears frozen corn, thawed, can be substituted for fresh corn.

1. Place beef, corn, bell pepper and onion in large resealable plastic food storage bag. Combine beer, chili sauce, mustard and garlic in small bowl; pour over beef and vegetables. Seal bag tightly, turning to coat. Marinate in refrigerator at least 1 hour or up to 8 hours, turning occasionally.

2. Prepare grill for direct cooking. Meanwhile, cover 1½ cups hickory chips with cold water; soak 20 minutes.

3. Drain beef and vegetables; reserve marinade. Alternately thread beef and vegetables onto 4 (12-inch) metal skewers. Brush with reserved marinade.

4. Drain hickory chips; sprinkle over coals. Place kabobs on grid. Grill kabobs, uncovered, over medium heat 5 minutes. Brush with reserved marinade; turn and brush again. Discard remaining marinade. Continue to grill 5 to 7 minutes for medium or until desired doneness.

5. Combine rice and chopped parsley; serve kabobs over rice mixture.

Makes 4 servings

Summer Sausage Dippers

    5 ounces sharp Cheddar cheese, cut into 1×½-inch chunks
  32 pimiento-stuffed green olives
    1 (9-ounce) HILLSHIRE FARM® Summer Sausage, cut into
        32 thick half-moon slices
    1 cup ketchup
  ½ cup apricot jam or preserves
    1 tablespoon cider vinegar
    2 teaspoons Worcestershire sauce

Secure 1 piece cheese and 1 olive onto 1 Summer Sausage slice with frilled toothpick; repeat with remaining cheese, olives and sausage. Arrange on platter. Cover and refrigerate until ready to serve. For dipping sauce, stir ketchup, jam, vinegar and Worcestershire sauce in small saucepan; heat over medium-low heat until warm and smooth. Serve sausage dippers with sauce.   ***Makes 8 servings***

Colorful Kabobs

  30 cocktail-size smoked sausages
  10 to 20 cherry or grape tomatoes
  10 to 20 large pimiento-stuffed green olives
    2 yellow bell peppers, cut into 1-inch squares
  ¼ cup butter or margarine, melted
      Lemon juice (optional)

1. Preheat oven to 450°F.

2. Thread 3 sausages onto 8-inch wooden skewer*, alternating with tomatoes, olives and bell peppers. Repeat on remaining nine skewers.

3. Place skewers on rack in shallow baking pan. Brush with melted butter and drizzle with lemon juice, if desired. Bake 4 to 6 minutes until hot.

    Makes 10 kabobs

*Soak skewers in water 20 minutes before using to prevent them from burning.

Kabobs Galore

Summer Sausage Dippers

Grilled Vegetable Kabobs

1 large red or green bell pepper
1 large zucchini
1 large yellow squash or additional zucchini
12 ounces large mushrooms
2 tablespoons olive oil
2 tablespoons red wine vinegar
1 package (7.2 ounces) RICE-A-RONI® Herb & Butter
1 large tomato, chopped
¼ cup grated Parmesan cheese

1. Cut red pepper into twelve 1-inch pieces. Cut zucchini and yellow squash crosswise into twelve ½-inch slices. Marinate red pepper, zucchini, yellow squash and mushrooms in combined oil and vinegar 15 minutes.

2. Alternately thread marinated vegetables onto 4 large metal skewers. Brush with any remaining oil mixture; set aside.

3. Prepare Rice-A-Roni® Mix as package directs.

4. While Rice-A-Roni® is simmering, grill kabobs over medium-low coals or broil 4 to 5 inches from heat 12 to 14 minutes or until tender and browned, turning once.

5. Stir tomato into rice. Serve rice topped with kabobs. Sprinkle with cheese.

Makes 4 servings

Kabobs Galore

Grilled Vegetable Kabobs

Glazed Chicken & Vegetable Skewers

12 small red or new potatoes, about 1½ inches in diameter (1 pound)
Golden Glaze (recipe follows)
1 pound boneless skinless chicken thighs or breasts, cut into 1-inch pieces
1 yellow or red bell pepper, cut into 1-inch pieces
½ small red onion, cut into 1-inch pieces
8 metal skewers (12-inches long)
Salt to taste

1. Prepare grill for direct cooking.

2. Cook potatoes in boiling water until almost tender, about 10 minutes (or, microwave at HIGH 3 to 4 minutes or until almost tender.) Rinse with cool water to stop the cooking.

3. Prepare Golden Glaze. Alternately thread chicken, potatoes, bell pepper and onion onto skewers. Brush glaze evenly over all sides of food.

4. Place skewers on grid over medium-hot coals. Grill, covered, 14 minutes for chicken breast or 16 minutes for chicken thighs or until chicken is cooked through and vegetables are crisp-tender, turning once. Season to taste with salt.

Makes 4 servings

Golden Glaze

¼ cup apricot or peach preserves
2 tablespoons spicy brown mustard*
2 cloves garlic, minced

*Dijon mustard can be substituted. Add ¼ teaspoon hot pepper sauce to glaze.

Combine all ingredients; mix well. Store tightly covered in refrigerator up to 2 weeks. Brush on chicken, pork or shrimp before grilling or broiling. (Marinade may be easily doubled for two uses.)

Makes about ⅓ cup glaze

Glazed Chicken & Vegetable Skewers

Barbecue Pork Kabobs

½ **cup ketchup**
¼ **cup white vinegar**
¼ **cup vegetable oil**
1 **tablespoon brown sugar**
1 **teaspoon dry mustard**
1 **clove garlic** *or* ½ **teaspoon garlic powder**
½ **teaspoon salt**
½ **teaspoon Worcestershire sauce**
¼ **teaspoon black pepper**
¼ **teaspoon hot pepper sauce (optional)**
4 **boneless pork chops, cut into 1½-inch cubes**
2 **green bell peppers, cut into chunks**
2 **onions, cut into chunks**
Skewers

1. In large resealable plastic food storage bag, combine ketchup, vinegar, oil, brown sugar, dry mustard, garlic, salt, Worcestershire, black pepper and hot pepper sauce, if desired; mix well. Remove ¼ cup marinade for basting. Add pork; seal bag. Marinate in refrigerator at least 1 hour.

2. Remove pork from marinade; discard used marinade. Alternately thread pork, bell peppers and onions onto skewers. Grill or broil skewers 15 to 20 minutes or until no longer pink in center, turning once and basting often with additional ¼ cup marinade. *Do not baste during last 5 minutes of cooking.* Discard any remaining marinade.

Makes 4 servings

Hint: *If using wooden skewers, soak in water 20 minutes before using to prevent scorching.*

Barbecue Pork Kabobs

Glazed Frank Kabobs

1 package (16 ounces) HEBREW NATIONAL® Quarter Pound
    Dinner Beef Franks, cut into 16 (1½-inch) pieces
1 small red onion, peeled, cut into ½-inch wedges
1 red bell pepper, seeded, cut into 1-inch pieces
1 green bell pepper, seeded, cut into 1-inch pieces
2 ears fresh corn, shucked *or* 4 small ears frozen corn on the
    cob, thawed, cut crosswise into 1-inch slices
½ cup chili sauce
3 tablespoons light brown sugar
2 tablespoons HEBREW NATIONAL® Deli Mustard

Prepare barbecue grill for direct cooking. Alternately thread franks and vegetables onto metal skewers. Set aside.

Combine chili sauce, sugar and mustard in small bowl; mix well. Place kabobs on grid over medium-hot coals. Brush with half of sauce. Grill, on covered grill, 5 minutes. Turn kabobs; brush with remaining sauce. Grill, covered, 5 to 7 minutes or until vegetables and franks are tender.

Makes 4 servings

Tip

When making kabobs, the food cooks and tastes better if loosely threaded on the skewers.

Glazed Frank Kabobs

91

Lemon-Garlic Shish Kabobs

1½ pounds well-trimmed boneless lamb leg, cubed
¼ cup olive oil
2 tablespoons fresh lemon juice
4 cloves garlic, minced
2 tablespoons chopped fresh oregano *or* 2 teaspoons dried
    oregano leaves
½ teaspoon salt
½ teaspoon black pepper
1 red or yellow bell pepper, cut into 1-inch pieces
1 small zucchini, cut into 1-inch pieces
1 yellow squash, cut into 1-inch pieces
1 small red onion, cut into ½-inch wedges
8 ounces large fresh button mushrooms, wiped clean and stems
    trimmed
Fresh oregano sprigs for garnish

1. Place lamb in large resealable plastic food storage bag. Combine oil, juice, garlic, chopped oregano, salt and black pepper in glass measuring cup; pour over lamb in bag. Close bag securely; turn to coat. Marinate lamb in refrigerator 1 to 4 hours, turning once.

2. Prepare grill for direct cooking.

3. Drain lamb, reserving marinade. Alternately thread lamb, bell pepper, zucchini, yellow squash, onion and mushrooms onto 12 (10-inch) metal skewers;* brush both sides with reserved marinade.

4. Place kabobs on grid. Grill, on covered grill, over medium-hot coals 6 minutes. Turn; continue to grill, covered, 5 to 7 minutes for medium or until desired doneness is reached. Garnish, if desired. Serve hot.

Makes 6 servings (2 kabobs each)

If using bamboo skewers, soak in cold water 10 to 15 minutes to prevent burning.

Lit'l Wiener Kabobs

30 **HILLSHIRE FARM® Lit'l Smokies**
 4 **dill pickles, cut into ¾-inch pieces**
 1 **pint cherry tomatoes**
 1 **can (4 ounces) button mushrooms, drained**
15 **large pimiento-stuffed green olives**
 1 **green bell pepper, cut into ¾-inch squares**
   Lemon Butter (recipe follows)

Preheat oven to 450°F.

Thread 2 Lit'l Smokies each onto 15 skewers alternating with pickles, tomatoes, mushrooms, olives and pepper. Place skewers on rack in broiler pan. Prepare Lemon Butter; brush skewers with butter. Bake 4 to 6 minutes or until hot. *Makes 15 hors d'oeuvres*

Lemon Butter

2 **tablespoons butter**
1 **teaspoon lemon juice**
  Dash hot pepper sauce

Combine all ingredients in small saucepan over medium-low heat; heat until butter is melted. *Makes about 2½ tablespoons*

Sausage-Bacon-Apricot Kabobs

**1 package BOB EVANS® Italian Grillin' Sausage
(approximately 5 links)
1 cup dried apricot halves
8 slices bacon
3 tablespoons apricot preserves
3 tablespoons lemon juice
1 tablespoon Dijon mustard
1 teaspoon Worcestershire sauce**

Precook sausage 10 minutes in gently boiling water. Drain and cut into
¾-inch slices. Alternate sausage and apricots on 8 wooden skewers,*
weaving bacon back and forth in ribbonlike fashion between them. Grill
or broil over medium-high heat 3 to 4 minutes on each side. Combine
preserves, lemon juice, mustard and Worcestershire in small bowl. Brush
preserves mixture on kabobs; continue grilling, turning and basting
frequently, until bacon is cooked through. Refrigerate leftovers.

Makes 8 kabobs

Soak wooden skewers in water 30 minutes before using to prevent burning.

Shrimp and Pineapple Kabobs

**8 ounces medium shrimp, peeled and deveined
½ cup pineapple juice
¼ teaspoon garlic powder
12 chunks canned pineapple
1 green bell pepper, cut into 1-inch pieces
¼ cup prepared chili sauce**

1. Combine shrimp, juice and garlic powder in bowl; toss to coat.
Marinate in refrigerator 30 minutes. Drain shrimp; discard marinade.

2. Alternately thread pineapple, pepper and shrimp onto 4 (10-inch)
skewers. Brush with chili sauce. Grill, 4 inches from hot coals, 5 minutes
or until shrimp are opaque, turning once and basting with chili sauce.

Makes 4 servings

Sausage-Bacon-Apricot Kabobs

Honey 'n' Spice Chicken Kabobs

1 medium green bell pepper, cut into 1-inch squares
2 boneless skinless chicken breasts, halved (about 1¼ pounds)
1 can (8 ounces) pineapple chunks, drained
½ cup HEINZ® 57 Sauce®
¼ cup honey

In small saucepan, blanch green pepper in boiling water 1 minute; drain. Cut each chicken breast half into 4 pieces. Alternately thread chicken, green pepper and pineapple onto skewers. In small bowl, combine 57 Sauce and honey. Brush kabobs with 57 Sauce mixture. Grill or broil kabobs, about 6 inches from heat, 12 to 14 minutes or until chicken is tender and no longer pink in center, turning and brushing with 57 Sauce mixture once.   ***Makes 4 servings***

Herbed Beef Kabobs

**1 cup LAWRY'S® Herb & Garlic Marinade with Lemon Juice,
    divided**
1 to 1½ pounds boneless, top sirloin beef, cut into chunks
12 mushrooms
2 medium green bell peppers, cut into 1½-inch squares
2 medium onions, cut into chunks
Skewers

In large resealable plastic bag, combine ¾ cup Herb & Garlic Marinade and beef. Seal bag and marinate in refrigerator for 30 minutes, turning several times. Remove beef from bag, discarding used marinade. On skewers, alternate beef with vegetables until all are used. Grill or broil to desired degree of doneness, about 10 to 14 minutes, brushing with remaining ¼ cup Marinade.   ***Makes 4 to 6 servings***

Hint: Soak wooden skewers in water for at least 20 minutes to help reduce burning.

Honey 'n' Spice Chicken Kabobs

Beef Kabobs with Apricot Glaze

1 can (15¼ ounces) DEL MONTE® Apricot Halves
1 tablespoon cornstarch
1 teaspoon Dijon mustard
½ teaspoon dried basil leaves
1 pound boneless beef top sirloin steak, cut into 1½-inch cubes
1 small green bell pepper, cut into ¾-inch pieces
4 medium mushrooms, cut in half
4 to 8 skewers*

To prevent burning of wooden skewers, soak skewers in water for 10 minutes before assembling kabobs.

1. Drain apricot syrup into small saucepan. Blend in cornstarch until dissolved. Cook over medium heat, stirring constantly, until thickened. Stir in mustard and basil. Set aside.

2. Thread beef, apricots, green pepper and mushrooms alternately onto skewers; brush with apricot syrup mixture. Grill kabobs over hot coals (or broil) about 5 minutes on each side or to desired doneness, brushing occasionally with additional syrup mixture. Garnish, if desired.

Makes 4 servings

Prep and Cook Time: 25 minutes

Tip Before you start grilling, let the charcoal burn for at least 30 minutes to form a gray ash over the coals. To check the temperature, count the number of seconds you can hold you hand over the grid before pulling it away. For a hot grill, you should only be able to hold you hand over the grid for 2 seconds.

Kabobs Galore

Beef Kabobs with Apricot Glaze

Spicy SPAM™ Kabobs

¼ cup lemon juice
3 tablespoons minced onion
1 tablespoon CARAPELLI® Extra Virgin Olive Oil
1 clove garlic, minced
1 teaspoon dried thyme leaves
½ teaspoon dried oregano leaves
¼ teaspoon crushed red pepper
16 pea pods
1 (8-ounce) can pineapple chunks packed in its own juice,
   drained
1 (12-ounce) can SPAM® Lite, cut into 24 cubes
1 red bell pepper, cut into 1-inch pieces
4 cups hot cooked white rice

Combine lemon juice, onion, olive oil, garlic, thyme, oregano and crushed red pepper in 13×9-inch dish. Wrap pea pods around pineapple chunks. Alternately thread SPAM® cubes, pineapple chunks and bell pepper pieces onto eight skewers. Place in dish with marinade. Cover and marinate 2 hours, turning occasionally. Grill kabobs over medium-hot coals 10 minutes, turning occasionally. Or, broil 5 inches from heat source 8 to 10 minutes, turning occasionally. Serve with rice.

Makes 4 servings

Kabobs Galore

Spicy SPAM™ Kabobs

Orange Mustard Ham Kabobs

¾ cup honey mustard barbecue sauce
½ cup orange marmalade
1½ pounds CURE 81® ham, cut into 1-inch cubes
2 small oranges, cut into 6 wedges each

In small bowl, combine barbecue sauce and marmalade; mix well. Remove ½ cup mixture for basting; reserve remaining mixture. Thread ham and orange wedges on skewers. Brush with ½ cup barbecue sauce mixture reserved for basting. Grill over medium-hot coals 10 minutes or until browned, turning frequently and basting with remaining barbecue mixture. Serve with reserved sauce mixture.   ***Makes 6 servings***

Alternate Method: Orange Mustard Ham Kabobs may be broiled *6 inches from heat source 10 minutes or until browned.*

Roasted Fruit Kabobs with Rum-Butter Sauce

¼ cup dark rum
1 tablespoon brown sugar
1 tablespoon sucralose-based sugar substitute
Pinch salt
1 tablespoon butter
2 cups fresh strawberries, washed, dried and halved
2 cups pineapple, cut into 1-inch pieces

1. Preheat oven to 425°F. Combine rum, brown sugar, sucralose and salt in a small saucepan. Bring to a simmer and simmer until bubbles form and alcohol evaporates. Remove from heat and swirl in butter. Stir until butter melts. Set aside.

2. Using 4 long metal skewers or 4 bamboo skewers that were soaked in water for 30 minutes, alternate strawberries and pineapple chunks on each skewer.

3. Place kabobs on a foil-lined cookie sheet. Brush with Rum-Butter Sauce. Roast for 5 minutes; turn, baste again with sauce and roast another 5 minutes or until fruit is soft.   ***Makes 4 servings***

Kabobs Galore

Orange Mustard Ham Kabob

Ginger Beef and Pineapple Kabobs

1 cup LAWRY'S® Thai Ginger Marinade with Lime Juice, divided
1 can (16 ounces) pineapple chunks, juice reserved
1½ pounds boneless beef top sirloin steak, cut into 1½-inch cubes
2 red bell peppers, cut into chunks
2 medium onions, cut into wedges

In large resealable plastic food storage bag, combine ½ cup Thai Ginger Marinade and 1 tablespoon pineapple juice; mix well. Add steak, bell peppers and onions; seal bag. Marinate in refrigerator at least 30 minutes. Remove steak and vegetables; discard used marinade. Alternately thread steak, vegetables and pineapple onto skewers. Grill or broil skewers 10 to 15 minutes or until desired doneness, turning once and basting often with additional ½ cup Thai Ginger Marinade. Do not baste during last 5 minutes of cooking. Discard any remaining marinade.

Makes 6 servings

Patio Chicken Kabobs

1 cup HUNT'S® Ketchup
¼ cup LA CHOY® Lite Soy Sauce
¼ cup firmly packed brown sugar
1 teaspoon crushed red pepper flakes
4 ready-to-cook chicken kabobs*

*These kabobs are available in grocer's meat department, or make your own by placing cubed chicken pieces with vegetables on skewers.

1. In small bowl combine *all* ingredients *except* kabobs; blend well.

2. Grill kabobs over medium-hot heat, about 10 minutes.

3. Baste chicken with marinade; continue cooking and basting for 10 minutes longer or until chicken is no longer pink in center.

Makes 4 kabobs

Kabobs Galore

Ginger Beef and Pineapple Kabobs

Hawaiian Shrimp Kabobs

1 can (6 ounces) pineapple juice
⅓ cup packed brown sugar
4 teaspoons cornstarch
1 tablespoon rice vinegar
1 tablespoon reduced-sodium soy sauce
1 clove garlic, minced
¼ teaspoon ground ginger
1 medium-size green bell pepper
1 medium-size red bell pepper
1 medium onion
1 cup fresh pineapple chunks
1 cup fresh mango or papaya chunks (1 mango, peeled, cut into
    bite-size pieces)
1 pound raw large shrimp, peeled, deveined
2½ cups hot cooked white rice
    Red onion rings and fresh herb sprigs (optional)

1. For sauce, combine juice, sugar, cornstarch, vinegar, soy sauce, garlic and ginger in saucepan. Cook over medium-high heat until mixture comes to a boil and thickens, stirring frequently; set aside.

2. Preheat broiler. Cut peppers and onion into 1-inch squares. Thread peppers, onion, pineapple, mango and shrimp onto 10 metal skewers. Place kabobs in large glass baking dish. Brush reserved sauce over kabobs.

3. Spray rack of broiler pan with nonstick cooking spray. Place kabobs on rack. Broil, 3 to 4 inches from heat, 3 minutes. Turn and brush with sauce; discard any remaining sauce. Broil 3 minutes more or until shrimp turn pink and opaque. Serve with rice. Garnish with onion rings and herbs, if desired.

Makes 5 servings

Grilled Sausage Kabobs with Apricot Mustard Sauce

¾ **cup apricot preserves**
¾ **cup Dijon mustard**
1 **pound smoked andouille or other pork sausage, cut into**
    1½-inch pieces
16 **dried apricot halves**
16 **medium whole mushrooms**

1. Prepare grill for direct grilling. Combine preserves and mustard in small bowl; mix well.

2. Thread sausage, apricots and mushrooms onto 4 skewers. Brush with ¼ of preserve mixture.

3. Grill over medium-hot coals 8 minutes, turning once. Baste with ½ of preserve mixture and continue grilling 2 minutes more, turning once, or until sausage is lightly browned. Serve kabobs with remaining ¼ of preserve mixture for dipping.   *Makes 4 servings*

Prep and Cook Time: 20 minutes

Note Andouille sausage is a spicy, smoked pork sausage often used in Cajun and Creole cooking. It makes a delicious addition to many other dishes.

Can-Opener Casseroles

'50s cooks discovered that canned soups made casseroles extra easy. Find such all-American favorites as Tuna Noodle Casserole, Beef Stroganoff and Chicken Divan.

Campbell's® Chicken Broccoli Divan

Campbell's® Chicken Broccoli Divan

1 pound fresh broccoli, cut into spears, cooked and drained, *or*
    1 package (about 10 ounces) frozen broccoli spears, cooked
    and drained
1½ cups cubed cooked chicken *or* turkey
  1 can (10¾ ounces) CAMPBELL'S® Condensed Broccoli Cheese
    Soup *or* Cream of Chicken Soup
  ⅓ cup milk
  ½ cup shredded Cheddar cheese (2 ounces, optional)
  2 tablespoons dry bread crumbs
  1 tablespoon margarine *or* butter, melted

1. In 9-inch pie plate or 2-quart shallow baking dish arrange broccoli and chicken. In small bowl mix soup and milk and pour over broccoli and chicken.

2. Sprinkle cheese over soup mixture. Mix bread crumbs with margarine and sprinkle over cheese.

3. Bake at 400°F. for 25 minutes or until hot.   ***Makes 4 servings***

Prep Time: 15 minutes
Cook Time: 25 minutes

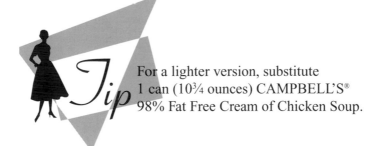

For a lighter version, substitute
1 can (10¾ ounces) CAMPBELL'S®
98% Fat Free Cream of Chicken Soup.

Can-Opener Casseroles

Escalloped Chicken

10 slices white bread, cubed
1½ cups cracker or dry bread crumbs, divided
4 cups cubed cooked chicken
3 cups chicken broth
1 cup chopped onion
1 cup chopped celery
1 can (8 ounces) sliced mushrooms, drained
1 jar (about 4 ounces) pimientos, diced
3 eggs, lightly beaten
Salt and black pepper
1 tablespoon margarine

1. Preheat oven to 350°F.

2. Combine bread cubes and 1 cup cracker crumbs in large mixing bowl. Add chicken, broth, onion, celery, mushrooms, pimientos and eggs; mix well. Season with salt and pepper; spoon into 2½-quart casserole.

3. Melt margarine in small saucepan. Add remaining ½ cup cracker crumbs and brown, stirring occasionally. Sprinkle crumbs over casserole.

4. Bake 1 hour or until hot and bubbly.   **Makes 6 servings**

Tip

When a recipe calls for chopped cooked chicken, it can be difficult to judge how much chicken to purchase. As a guideline, two whole chicken breasts (about 10 ounces each) will yield about 2 cups of chopped cooked chicken; one broiling/frying chicken (about 3 pounds) will yield about 2½ cups chopped cooked chicken.

Can-Opener Casseroles

Escalloped Chicken

Salmon Casserole

2 tablespoons margarine or butter
2 cups sliced mushrooms
1½ cups chopped carrots
1 cup chopped celery
1 cup frozen peas
½ cup chopped onion
½ cup chopped red bell pepper
1 tablespoon chopped fresh parsley
1 clove garlic, minced
1 teaspoon salt
½ teaspoon black pepper
½ teaspoon dried basil leaves
4 cups cooked rice
1 can (14 ounces) red salmon, drained and flaked
1 can (10¾ ounces) condensed cream of mushroom soup, undiluted
2 cups (8 ounces) grated Cheddar or American cheese
½ cup sliced black olives

1. Preheat oven to 350°F. Spray 2-quart casserole with nonstick cooking spray; set aside.

2. Melt margarine in large skillet or Dutch oven over medium heat. Add mushrooms, carrots, celery, peas, onion, bell pepper, parsley, garlic, salt, black pepper and basil; cook and stir 10 minutes or until vegetables are tender. Add rice, salmon, soup and cheese; mix well.

3. Transfer to prepared casserole. Sprinkle olives over top. Bake 30 minutes or until hot and bubbly.   ***Makes 8 servings***

Salmon Casserole

Cheesy Broccoli Bake

......●●●

1 (10-ounce) package frozen chopped broccoli
1 (10¾-ounce) can condensed Cheddar cheese soup
½ cup sour cream
2 cups (12 ounces) chopped CURE 81® ham
2 cups cooked rice
½ cup soft, torn bread crumbs
1 tablespoon butter or margarine, melted

Heat oven to 350°F. Cook broccoli according to package directions; drain. Combine soup and sour cream. Stir in broccoli, ham and rice. Spoon into 1½-quart casserole. Combine bread crumbs and butter; sprinkle over casserole. Bake 30 to 35 minutes or until thoroughly heated. **Makes 4 to 6 servings**

Chicken Veggie Casserole

......●●●

1 can (10¾ ounces) condensed cheese soup, undiluted
1 cup milk
1½ cups cooked chicken, cut into bite-size pieces
1 can (about 16 ounces) sliced potatoes
1 can (about 15 ounces) mixed vegetables
2 cups biscuit mix
2 tablespoons mayonnaise
1 egg

1. Preheat oven to 400°F.

2. Bring soup and milk to a boil over medium-high heat in large saucepan, stirring constantly. Stir in chicken, potatoes and vegetables. Pour into 13×9-inch baking dish.

3. Combine biscuit mix, mayonnaise and egg in medium bowl; mix just until crumbly. Sprinkle over chicken mixture.

4. Bake, uncovered, 30 minutes or until browned and bubbly.

Makes 4 to 6 servings

Can-Opener Casseroles

Cheesy Broccoli Bake

4 BAYS® English Muffins, split
2 packages (10 ounces each) frozen Welsh rarebit (Cheddar cheese sauce)
2 teaspoons prepared honey mustard
8 slices ripe tomato
8 slices cut bacon, preferably applewood smoked, halved crosswise, cooked crisp
3 tablespoons chopped chives

Lightly toast muffin halves; place open-faced on four serving plates. Cook rarebit according to package directions; stir in mustard. Top muffin halves with sliced tomatoes. Arrange bacon over tomatoes in a crisscross fashion. Spoon rarebit evenly over muffin halves and sprinkle with chives.

Makes 4 servings

Variation: For a heartier rarebit, place sliced deli smoked turkey breast on muffin halves before topping with cheese, tomato and chives.

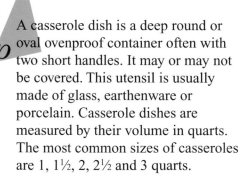

Tip

A casserole dish is a deep round or oval ovenproof container often with two short handles. It may or may not be covered. This utensil is usually made of glass, earthenware or porcelain. Casserole dishes are measured by their volume in quarts. The most common sizes of casseroles are 1, 1½, 2, 2½ and 3 quarts.

Bays® Welsh Rarebit

Turkey & Green Bean Casserole

···•••

¼ cup slivered almonds
1 package (7 ounces) herb-seasoned stuffing cubes
¾ cup reduced-sodium chicken broth
1 can (10¾ ounces) condensed cream of mushroom soup
¼ cup milk or half-and-half
¼ teaspoon black pepper
1 package (10 ounces) frozen French-style green beans, thawed
    and drained
2 cups (½-inch-thick) deli turkey breast cubes or cooked turkey
    or chicken

1. Preheat oven to 350°F. Spray 11×7-inch baking dish with nonstick cooking spray.

2. Spread almonds in single layer on baking sheet. Bake 5 minutes or until golden brown, stirring frequently. Set aside.

3. Arrange stuffing cubes in prepared dish; drizzle with broth. Stir to coat bread cubes with broth.

4. Combine soup, milk and pepper in large bowl. Add green beans and turkey; stir until combined. Spoon over stuffing cubes; top with almonds. Bake, uncovered, 30 to 35 minutes or until heated through.

Makes 4 servings

Tip

Many casserole dishes are ideal for microwave cooking and some are suitable for use on the stovetop. Check the manufacturer's label to determine if a dish can be used in these ways.

Turkey & Green Bean Casserole

Seafood Newburg Casserole

· · ● ● ● ●

1 can (10¾ ounces) condensed cream of shrimp soup, undiluted
½ cup half-and-half
1 tablespoon dry sherry
¼ teaspoon ground red pepper
3 cups cooked rice
2 cans (6 ounces each) lump crabmeat, drained
¼ pound medium shrimp, peeled and deveined
¼ pound bay scallops
1 jar (4 ounces) pimientos, drained and chopped
¼ cup finely chopped parsley

1. Preheat oven to 350°F. Spray 2½-quart casserole with nonstick cooking spray.

2. Whisk together soup, half-and-half, sherry and red pepper in large bowl until combined. Add rice, crabmeat, shrimp, scallops and pimientos; toss well.

3. Transfer to prepared casserole; sprinkle with parsley. Cover and bake about 25 minutes or until shrimp and scallops are opaque.

Makes 6 servings

Note

A Newburg is a rich dish of cooked shellfish such as crab and shrimp in a cream sauce. It is often served in a chafing dish on buffets.

Seafood Newburg Casserole

Veg•All® Beef & Cheddar Bake

····●●●●

2 cans (15 ounces each) VEG•ALL® Original Mixed Vegetables,
    drained
3 cups shredded Cheddar cheese
2 cups cooked elbow macaroni
1 pound extra-lean ground beef, cooked and drained
½ cup chopped onion
¼ teaspoon pepper

1. Preheat oven to 350°F.

2. In large mixing bowl, combine Veg•All, cheese, macaroni, ground
beef, onion and pepper; mix well. Pour mixture into large casserole.

3. Bake for 30 to 35 minutes. Serve hot.   ***Makes 4 to 6 servings***

Classic Hamburger Casserole

····●●●●

1 pound ground beef
1 package (9 ounces) frozen cut green beans, thawed and
    drained
1 can (10¾ ounces) condensed tomato soup
¼ cup water
½ teaspoon seasoned salt
⅛ teaspoon pepper
2 cups hot mashed potatoes
1⅓ cups *French's*® French Fried Onions, divided
½ cup (2 ounces) shredded Cheddar cheese

Preheat oven to 350°F. In medium skillet, brown ground beef; drain. Stir
in green beans, soup, water and seasonings; pour into 1½-quart casserole.
In medium bowl, combine mashed potatoes and ⅔ *cup* French Fried
Onions. Spoon potato mixture in mounds around edge of casserole.
Bake, uncovered, at 350°F for 25 minutes or until heated through. Top
potatoes with cheese and remaining ⅔ *cup* onions; bake, uncovered,
5 minutes or until onions are golden brown.   ***Makes 4 to 6 servings***

Veg•All® Beef & Cheddar Bake

Beef Stroganoff Casserole

. . . ● ● ● ●

1 pound lean ground beef
¼ teaspoon salt
⅛ teaspoon black pepper
1 teaspoon vegetable oil
8 ounces sliced mushrooms
1 large onion, chopped
3 cloves garlic, minced
¼ cup dry white wine
1 can (10¾ ounces) condensed cream of mushroom soup
½ cup sour cream
1 tablespoon Dijon mustard
4 cups cooked egg noodles
Chopped fresh parsley (optional)

1. Preheat oven to 350°F. Spray 13×9-inch baking dish with nonstick cooking spray.

2. Place beef in large skillet; season with salt and pepper. Brown beef over medium-high heat until no longer pink, stirring to separate meat. Drain fat from skillet; set aside.

3. Heat oil in same skillet over medium-high heat until hot. Add mushrooms, onion and garlic; cook and stir 2 minutes or until onion is tender. Add wine. Reduce heat to medium-low and simmer 3 minutes. Remove from heat; stir in soup, sour cream and mustard until well combined. Return beef to skillet.

4. Place noodles in prepared dish. Pour beef mixture over noodles; stir until noodles are well coated. Bake, uncovered, 30 minutes or until heated through. Sprinkle with parsley, if desired.   ***Makes 6 servings***

Beef Stroganoff Casserole

Chicken Divan Casserole

· · ○ ○ ● ●

1 cup uncooked rice
1 cup coarsely shredded carrots*
  Nonstick cooking spray
4 boneless skinless chicken breasts
2 tablespoons butter or margarine
3 tablespoons all-purpose flour
¼ teaspoon salt
  Black pepper to taste
1 cup fat-free chicken broth
½ cup milk or half-and-half
¼ cup white wine
⅓ cup plus 2 tablespoons grated Parmesan cheese, divided
1 pound frozen broccoli florets

*Coarsely shredded carrots are available in the produce sections of many large supermarkets or shred them on a hand-held grater.

1. Preheat oven to 350°F. Lightly grease 12×8-inch baking dish.

2. Prepare rice according to package directions. Stir in carrots. Spread mixture into prepared baking dish.

3. Spray large skillet with cooking spray. Heat over medium-high heat. Brown chicken breasts about 2 minutes on each side. Arrange over rice.

4. To prepare sauce, melt butter in 2-quart saucepan over medium heat. Whisk in flour, salt and pepper; cook and stir 1 minute. Gradually whisk in broth and milk. Cook and stir until mixture comes to a boil. Reduce heat; simmer for 2 minutes. Stir in wine. Remove from heat. Stir in ⅓ cup cheese.

5. Arrange broccoli around chicken. Pour sauce over chicken and broccoli. Sprinkle remaining 2 tablespoons cheese over chicken.

6. Cover with foil; bake 30 minutes. Remove foil. Bake 10 to 15 minutes or until chicken is no longer pink in center and broccoli is hot.

Makes 6 servings

Chicken Divan Casserole

Shrimp Noodle Supreme

....●●●

1 package (8 ounces) spinach noodles, cooked and drained
1 package (3 ounces) cream cheese, cubed and softened
1½ pounds medium shrimp, peeled and deveined
½ cup butter, softened
Salt and black pepper
1 can (10¾ ounces) condensed cream of mushroom soup
1 cup sour cream
½ cup half-and-half
½ cup mayonnaise
1 tablespoon snipped chives
1 tablespoon chopped fresh parsley
½ teaspoon Dijon mustard
¾ cup (6 ounces) shredded sharp Cheddar cheese

1. Preheat oven to 325°F.

2. Combine noodles and cream cheese in medium bowl. Spread noodle mixture in bottom of greased 13×9-inch glass casserole.

3. Cook shrimp in butter in large skillet over medium-high heat until pink and tender, about 5 minutes. Season to taste with salt and pepper. Spread shrimp over noodles.

4. Combine soup, sour cream, half-and-half, mayonnaise, chives, parsley and mustard in another medium bowl. Spread over shrimp. Sprinkle Cheddar cheese over top.

5. Bake 25 minutes or until hot and cheese is melted. Garnish, if desired.

Makes 6 servings

Can-Opener Casseroles

Shrimp Noodle Supreme

Sunny Day Casserole

· · ● ● ● ●

1 jar (8 ounces) pasteurized processed cheese spread, melted
¾ cup milk
4 cups diced potatoes, partially cooked
2 cups diced HILLSHIRE FARM® Ham
1 package (16 ounces) frozen mixed vegetables, thawed
½ cup chopped onion
1 cup (4 ounces) shredded Swiss, Cheddar or Monterey Jack
    cheese
1 cup cracker crumbs

Preheat oven to 350°F.

Combine cheese spread and milk in large bowl. Stir in potatoes, Ham,
mixed vegetables and onion. Pour into medium casserole. Bake, covered,
45 minutes, stirring occasionally. Sprinkle Swiss cheese and cracker
crumbs over top. Bake, uncovered, until Swiss cheese is melted.

Makes 6 servings

Tasty Turkey Divan

· · ● ● ● ●

1 can (10¾ ounces) condensed cream of mushroom soup
¾ cup milk
2 cups cubed cooked turkey
1 package (10 ounces) frozen broccoli florets, thawed
1⅓ cups *French's®* French Fried Onions, divided
4 to 5 slices buttered, toasted white bread
1 cup grated Parmesan cheese

1. Preheat oven to 350°F. Combine soup and milk in medium bowl; stir in
turkey, broccoli and ⅔ *cup* French Fried Onions.

2. Place toast slices in bottom of greased 2-quart shallow baking dish,
cutting to fit if necessary. Spoon turkey mixture on top.

3. Bake 25 minutes or until mixture is heated through. Sprinkle with
cheese and remaining onions; bake 5 minutes or until cheese is melted
and onions are golden.

Makes 6 servings

Sunny Day Casserole

Johnnie Marzetti

......●●●

1 tablespoon CRISCO® Oil*
1 cup chopped celery
1 cup chopped onion
1 medium green bell pepper, chopped
1 pound ground beef round
1 can (14½ ounces) Italian-style stewed tomatoes, undrained
1 can (8 ounces) tomato sauce
1 can (6 ounces) tomato paste
1 cup water
1 bay leaf
1½ teaspoons dried basil leaves
1¼ teaspoons salt
¼ teaspoon black pepper
1 package (12 ounces) egg noodles, cooked and well drained
½ cup plain dry bread crumbs
1 cup (4 ounces) shredded sharp Cheddar cheese

*Use your favorite Crisco Oil product.

1. Heat oven to 375°F. Oil 12½×8½×2-inch baking dish lightly. Place cooling rack on countertop.

2. Heat oil in large skillet on medium heat. Add celery, onion and green pepper. Cook and stir until tender. Remove vegetables from skillet. Set aside. Add meat to skillet. Cook until browned, stirring occasionally. Return vegetables to skillet. Add tomatoes, tomato sauce, tomato paste, water, bay leaf, basil, salt and black pepper. Reduce heat to low. Simmer 5 minutes, stirring occasionally. Remove bay leaf.

3. Place noodles in baking dish. Spoon meat mixture over noodles. Sprinkle with bread crumbs and cheese.

4. Bake at 375°F for 15 to 20 minutes or until cheese melts. *Do not overbake.* Remove baking dish to cooling rack. Garnish, if desired.

Makes 8 servings

Johnnie Marzetti

Lasagna Supreme

8 ounces uncooked lasagna noodles
½ pound ground beef
½ pound mild Italian sausage, casings removed
1 medium onion, chopped
2 cloves garlic, minced
1 can (14½ ounces) whole peeled tomatoes, undrained and
    chopped
1 can (6 ounces) tomato paste
2 teaspoons dried basil leaves
1 teaspoon dried marjoram leaves
1 can (4 ounces) sliced mushrooms, drained
2 eggs
2 cups (16 ounces) cream-style cottage cheese
¾ cup grated Parmesan cheese, divided
2 tablespoons dried parsley flakes
½ teaspoon salt
½ teaspoon black pepper
2 cups (8 ounces) shredded Cheddar cheese
3 cups (12 ounces) shredded mozzarella cheese

1. Cook lasagna noodles according to package directions; drain.

2. Cook meats, onion and garlic in large skillet over medium-high heat until meat is brown, stirring to separate meat. Drain drippings from skillet.

3. Add tomatoes with juice, tomato paste, basil and marjoram. Reduce heat to low. Cover; simmer 15 minutes, stirring often. Stir in mushrooms; set aside.

4. Preheat oven to 375°F. Beat eggs in large bowl; add cottage cheese, ½ cup Parmesan cheese, parsley, salt and pepper. Mix well.

5. Place half the noodles in bottom of greased 13×9-inch baking pan. Spread half the cottage cheese mixture over noodles, then half the meat mixture and half the Cheddar cheese and mozzarella cheese. Repeat layers. Sprinkle with remaining ¼ cup Parmesan cheese.

6. Bake lasagna 40 to 45 minutes or until bubbly. Let stand 10 minutes before cutting.   *Makes 8 to 10 servings*

Lasagna Supreme

Easy Three Cheese Tuna Soufflé

· · · ● ● ●

4 cups large croutons*
2½ cups milk
4 large eggs
1 can (10¾ ounces) cream of celery soup
3 cups shredded cheese, use a combination of Cheddar,
   Monterey Jack and Swiss
1 (7-ounce) pouch of STARKIST® Premium Albacore or Chunk
   Light Tuna
1 tablespoon butter or margarine
½ cup chopped celery
½ cup finely chopped onion
¼ pound mushrooms, sliced

*Use garlic and herb or ranch-flavored croutons.

In bottom of lightly greased 13×9-inch baking dish, arrange croutons. In medium bowl, beat together milk, eggs and soup; stir in cheeses and tuna. In small skillet, melt butter over medium heat. Add celery, onion and mushrooms; sauté until onion is soft.

Spoon sautéed vegetables over croutons; pour egg-tuna mixture over top. Cover; refrigerate overnight. Remove from refrigerator 1 hour before baking; bake in 325°F oven 45 to 50 minutes or until hot and bubbly.

Makes 8 servings

Prep Time: 60 minutes

Easy Three Cheese Tuna Soufflé

Creamy SPAM™ Broccoli Casserole

Nonstick cooking spray
1 (7-ounce) package elbow macaroni
2 cups frozen cut broccoli, thawed and drained
1 (12-ounce) can SPAM® Lite, cubed
½ cup chopped red bell pepper
2 cups skim milk
2 tablespoons cornstarch
¼ teaspoon black pepper
1 cup (4 ounces) shredded fat-free Cheddar cheese
¾ cup soft bread crumbs
2 teaspoons margarine, melted

Heat oven to 350°F. Spray 2-quart casserole with nonstick cooking spray. Cook macaroni according to package directions; drain. In prepared casserole, combine macaroni, broccoli, SPAM® and bell pepper. In small saucepan, stir together milk, cornstarch and black pepper until cornstarch is dissolved. Bring to a boil, stirring constantly, until thickened. Reduce heat to low. Add cheese; stir until melted. Stir sauce into SPAM™ mixture. Combine bread crumbs and margarine; sprinkle on top of casserole. Bake 40 minutes or until thoroughly heated.

Makes 8 servings

Tip If you don't have bread crumbs available for a casserole topping, substitute cracker crumbs, crushed corn or potato chips or crushed salad croutons. Add herbs, paprika or ground red pepper to liven up a crumb topping.

Creamy SPAM™ Broccoli Casserole

Beef Stroganoff

• • • • • •

12 ounces uncooked wide egg noodles
1 can (10¾ ounces) condensed cream of mushroom soup,
    undiluted
1 cup (8 ounces) sour cream
1 package (1¼ ounces) dry onion soup mix
1¼ to 1½ pounds 90% lean ground beef
½ (10-ounce) package frozen peas, thawed

1. Place 3 quarts water in 8-quart stockpot; bring to a boil over high heat. Stir in noodles; boil, uncovered, 6 minutes or until tender. Drain.

2. Meanwhile, place mushroom soup, sour cream and onion soup mix in medium bowl. Stir until blended; set aside.

3. Brown meat in large skillet over high heat 6 to 8 minutes or until meat is no longer pink, stirring to separate meat. Pour off drippings. Reduce heat to low. Add soup mixture; stir over low heat until bubbly.

4. Stir in peas; heat through. Serve over noodles.   ***Makes 6 servings***

Prep and Cook Time: 20 minutes

Note

With this easy version of Beef Stroganoff, you can have dinner on the table in 30 minutes. Add a tossed green salad or fresh fruit for a nutritious meal your family will love.

Beef Stroganoff

Chicken Tetrazzini

···●●●●●

8 ounces uncooked vermicelli, broken in half
1 can (10¾ ounces) condensed cream of mushroom soup, undiluted
¼ cup half-and-half
3 tablespoons dry sherry
½ teaspoon salt
⅛ to ¼ teaspoon red pepper flakes
2 cups chopped cooked chicken breasts (about ¾ pound)
1 cup frozen peas
½ cup grated Parmesan cheese
1 cup fresh coarse bread crumbs
2 tablespoons margarine or butter, melted
Chopped fresh basil (optional)

1. Preheat oven to 375°F. Spray 8-inch square baking dish with nonstick cooking spray.

2. Cook pasta according to package directions until al dente. Drain and set aside.

3. Meanwhile, combine soup, half-and-half, sherry, salt and pepper flakes in large bowl. Stir in chicken, peas and cheese. Add pasta to chicken mixture; stir until pasta is well coated. Pour into prepared dish.

4. Combine bread crumbs and margarine in small bowl. Sprinkle evenly over casserole. Bake, uncovered, 25 to 30 minutes or until heated through and crumbs are golden brown. Sprinkle with basil, if desired.

Makes 4 servings

Note Have rotisserie chicken from your local supermarket for dinner one night and use 2 cups leftover chicken to make Tetrazzini the next.

Can-Opener Casseroles

Chicken Tetrazzini

Campbell's® Tuna Noodle Casserole

1 can (10¾ ounces) CAMPBELL'S® Condensed Cream of
    Mushroom Soup *or* 98% Fat Free Cream of Mushroom Soup
½ cup milk
2 tablespoons chopped pimiento (optional)
1 cup cooked peas
2 cans (about 6 ounces *each*) tuna, drained and flaked
2 cups hot cooked medium egg noodles (about 1 cup uncooked)
2 tablespoons dry bread crumbs
1 tablespoon margarine *or* butter, melted

1. In 1½-quart casserole mix soup, milk, pimiento, peas, tuna and
noodles. Bake at 400°F. for 20 minutes or until hot.

2. Stir. Mix bread crumbs with margarine and sprinkle over noodle
mixture. Bake 5 minutes more.   *Makes 4 servings*

Prep Time: 15 minutes
Cook Time: 25 minutes

Tip For a cheesy bread topping, mix
¼ cup shredded Cheddar cheese
(about 1 ounce) with bread crumbs
and margarine. For a change of taste,
substitute 1 can (10¾ ounces)
CAMPBELL'S® Condensed Cream of
Celery Soup *or* 98% Fat Free Cream
of Celery Soup for Cream of
Mushroom Soup.

Campbell's® Tuna Noodle Casserole

Chicken Rice Casserole

4 tablespoons butter, divided
4 boneless skinless chicken breasts
1½ cups uncooked converted rice
6 ounces HILLSHIRE FARM® Lit'l Smokies
1 can (about 14 ounces) cream of chicken soup
1 can (about 14 ounces) cream of celery soup
1 cup sliced mushrooms
½ cup dry sherry
  Bread crumbs
  Cheddar cheese
  Slivered almonds

Preheat oven to 275°F.

Melt 2 tablespoons butter in large skillet over medium-high heat. Add chicken; sauté until cooked through, about 7 minutes on each side. Remove chicken and cut into bite-size pieces.

Place rice on bottom of medium casserole; add chicken, Lit'l Smokies, soups, ¾ cup water, mushrooms, sherry and remaining 2 tablespoons butter. Bake, covered, 2½ hours. Top casserole with bread crumbs, cheese and almonds. Broil until golden brown and cheese is melted.

Makes 6 to 8 servings

Tip

A major pitfall of casseroles destined for the freezer is overcooking. Simply undercook any pasta or rice; it will cook through when the casserole is reheated.

Chicken Rice Casserole

Cheesy Country SPAM™ Puff

6 slices white bread, torn into small pieces
1¼ cups milk
3 eggs
1 tablespoon spicy mustard
½ teaspoon garlic powder
½ teaspoon paprika
1 (12-ounce) can SPAM® Classic, cubed
2 cups (8 ounces) shredded sharp Cheddar cheese, divided
½ cup chopped onion
½ cup (2 ounces) shredded Monterey Jack cheese

Heat oven to 375°F. In large bowl, combine bread, milk, eggs, mustard, garlic powder and paprika. Beat at medium speed of electric mixer 1 minute or until smooth. Stir in SPAM®, 1 cup Cheddar cheese and onion. Pour into greased 12×8-inch baking dish. Bake 25 minutes. Top with remaining 1 cup Cheddar cheese and Monterey Jack cheese. Bake 5 minutes longer or until cheese is melted. Let stand 10 minutes before serving. **_Makes 8 servings_**

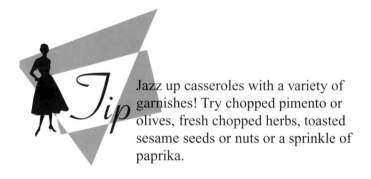

Tip — Jazz up casseroles with a variety of garnishes! Try chopped pimento or olives, fresh chopped herbs, toasted sesame seeds or nuts or a sprinkle of paprika.

Cheesy Country SPAM™ Puff

Tuna Noodle Casserole

· · • • • •

7 ounces uncooked elbow macaroni
2 tablespoons margarine or butter
¾ cup chopped onion
½ cup thinly sliced celery
½ cup finely chopped red bell pepper
2 tablespoons all-purpose flour
1 teaspoon salt
⅛ teaspoon white pepper
1½ cups milk
1 can (6 ounces) albacore tuna in water, drained
½ cup grated Parmesan cheese, divided
Fresh dill sprigs (optional)

1. Preheat oven to 375°F. Spray 8-inch square baking dish with nonstick cooking spray.

2. Cook pasta according to package directions until al dente. Drain and set aside.

3. Meanwhile, melt margarine in large deep skillet over medium heat. Add onion; cook and stir 3 minutes. Add celery and bell pepper; cook and stir 3 minutes. Sprinkle flour, salt and white pepper over vegetables; cook and stir 1 minute. Gradually stir in milk; cook and stir until thickened. Remove from heat.

4. Add pasta, tuna and ¼ cup cheese to skillet; stir until pasta is well coated. Pour tuna mixture into prepared dish; sprinkle evenly with remaining ¼ cup cheese.

5. Bake, uncovered, 20 to 25 minutes or until hot and bubbly. Garnish with dill, if desired.

Makes 4 servings

Tuna Noodle Casserole

Meatball Stroganoff with Rice

Meatballs
- 1½ pounds ground beef round
- 1 egg, lightly beaten
- ⅓ cup plain dry bread crumbs
- 1 tablespoon Worcestershire sauce
- 1 teaspoon salt
- ¼ teaspoon pepper
- 2 tablespoons CRISCO® Oil*

Sauce
- 1 tablespoon CRISCO® Oil
- ½ pound mushrooms, sliced
- 2 tablespoons all-purpose flour
- 1 teaspoon ketchup
- 1 can (10½ ounces) condensed, double strength beef broth
      (bouillon), undiluted**
- ½ (1-ounce) envelope dry onion soup mix (about 2 tablespoons)
- 1 cup sour cream
- 4 cups hot cooked rice

*Use your favorite Crisco Oil product.

**1¼ cups reconstituted beef broth made with double amount of very low sodium beef broth granules can be substituted for beef broth (bouillon).

1. For meatballs, combine meat, egg, bread crumbs, Worcestershire sauce, salt and pepper in large bowl. Mix until well blended. Shape into eighteen 2-inch meatballs.

2. Heat 2 tablespoons oil in large skillet on medium heat. Add meatballs. Brown on all sides. Reduce heat to low. Cook 10 minutes. Remove meatballs from skillet.

3. For sauce, add 1 tablespoon oil to skillet. Add mushrooms. Cook and stir 4 minutes. Remove skillet from heat.

4. Stir in flour and ketchup until blended. Stir in broth gradually. Add soup mix. Return to heat. Bring to a boil on medium heat. Reduce heat to low. Simmer 2 minutes. Return meatballs to skillet. Heat thoroughly, stirring occasionally.

5. Stir in sour cream. Heat but do not bring to a boil. Serve over hot rice. Garnish, if desired.

Makes 6 servings

Can-Opener Casseroles

Meatball Stroganoff with Rice

Lit'l Smokies 'n' Macaroni 'n' Cheese

1 package (7¼ ounces) macaroni and cheese mix, prepared
    according to package directions
1 pound HILLSHIRE FARM® Lit'l Smokies
1 can (10¾ ounces) condensed cream of celery or mushroom
    soup, undiluted
⅓ cup milk
1 tablespoon minced parsley (optional)
1 cup (4 ounces) shredded Cheddar cheese

Preheat oven to 350°F.

Combine prepared macaroni and cheese, Lit'l Smokies, soup, milk and
parsley, if desired, in medium bowl. Pour into small greased casserole.
Sprinkle Cheddar cheese over top. Bake, uncovered, 20 minutes or until
heated through. *Makes 8 servings*

Swissed Ham and Noodles Casserole

2 tablespoons butter
½ cup chopped onion
½ cup chopped green pepper
1 can (10½ ounces) condensed cream of mushroom soup
1 cup dairy sour cream
1 package (8 ounces) medium noodles, cooked and drained
2 cups (8 ounces) shredded Wisconsin Swiss cheese
2 cups cubed cooked ham (about ¾ pound)

In 1-quart saucepan, melt butter; sauté onion and green pepper. Remove
from heat; stir in soup and sour cream. In buttered 2-quart casserole,
layer ⅓ of the noodles, ⅓ of the Swiss cheese, ⅓ of the ham and ½ soup
mixture. Repeat layers, ending with final ⅓ layer of noodles, cheese and
ham. Bake in preheated 350°F oven 30 to 45 minutes or until heated
through. *Makes 6 to 8 servings*

Favorite recipe from Wisconsin Milk Marketing Board

Lit'l Smokies 'n' Macaroni 'n' Cheese

Classic Sides

Return to the gelatin craze and surprise your family with a popular molded salad. And don't forget such original classics as Green Bean Casserole and Three Bean Salad.

Saucy Vegetable Casserole

Saucy Vegetable Casserole

● ● ● ● ● ● ● ● ●

2 bags (16 ounces each) frozen mixed vegetables (broccoli, cauliflower, carrots), thawed
2 cups *French's*® French Fried Onions, divided
1 package (16 ounces) pasteurized process cheese, cut into ¼-inch slices

1. Preheat oven to 350°F. Combine vegetables and *1 cup* French Fried Onions in shallow 3-quart baking dish. Top evenly with cheese slices.

2. Bake 15 minutes or until hot and cheese is almost melted; stir. Top with remaining onions and bake 5 minutes or until onions are golden.

Makes 8 servings

*Variation: For added Cheddar flavor, substitute **French's**® **Cheddar French Fried Onions** for the original flavor.*

Prep Time: 5 minutes
Cook Time: 20 minutes

The Original Potato Salad

● ● ● ● ● ● ● ● ●

1 cup HELLMANN'S® or BEST FOODS® Real Mayonnaise Dressing
2 tablespoons vinegar
1½ teaspoons salt
1 teaspoon sugar
¼ teaspoon freshly ground pepper
2 pounds potatoes, peeled, cubed and cooked (about 4 cups)
1 cup thinly sliced celery
½ cup chopped onion
2 hard-cooked eggs, diced

1. In large bowl, blend mayonnaise, vinegar, salt, sugar and pepper.

2. Stir in potatoes, celery, onion and eggs.

3. Cover and chill to blend flavors.

Makes about 8 servings

Classic Sides

Spinach & Egg Casserole

1 box (10 ounces) BIRDS EYE® frozen Chopped Spinach
1 can (15 ounces) Cheddar cheese soup
1 tablespoon mustard
½ pound deli ham, cut into ¼-inch cubes
4 hard-boiled eggs, chopped or sliced

- Preheat oven to 350°F.

- In large saucepan, cook spinach according to package directions; drain well.

- Stir in soup, mustard and ham.

- Pour into 9×9-inch baking pan. Top with eggs.

- Bake 15 to 20 minutes or until heated through.   *Makes 4 servings*

Serving Suggestion: Sprinkle with paprika for added color.

Birds Eye Idea: Cook eggs the day before and refrigerate. They will be much easier to peel.

Prep Time: 10 minutes
Cook Time: 15 to 20 minutes

Fruited Coleslaw

½ head green cabbage, shredded
1 cup shredded red cabbage
1 cup walnuts, toasted
2 red apples, sliced
1½ cups prepared HIDDEN VALLEY® The Original Ranch® Dressing

In large bowl, combine all ingredients. Toss gently. Cover and refrigerate until ready to serve.   *Makes 4 to 6 servings*

Spinach & Egg Casserole

Country Bean Soup

1¼ cups dried navy beans or lima beans, rinsed and drained
4 ounces salt pork or fully cooked ham, chopped
¼ cup chopped onion
½ teaspoon dried oregano leaves
¼ teaspoon salt
¼ teaspoon ground ginger
¼ teaspoon dried sage
¼ teaspoon black pepper
2 cups fat-free (skim) milk
2 tablespoons butter

1. Place navy beans in large saucepan; add enough water to cover beans. Bring to a boil; reduce heat and simmer 2 minutes. Remove from heat; cover and let stand 1 hour. (Or, cover beans with water and soak overnight.)

2. Drain beans and return to saucepan. Stir in 2½ cups water, salt pork, onion, oregano, salt, ginger, sage and pepper. Bring to a boil; reduce heat. Cover and simmer 2 to 2½ hours or until beans are tender. (If necessary, add more water during cooking.) Add milk and butter, stirring until mixture is heated through and butter is melted. Season with additional salt and pepper, if desired. **Makes 6 servings**

Tip When planning your shopping list, use the following equivalents to make sure you purchase the correct amount. 1 pound dried beans equals 2½ cups uncooked and 5½ to 6½ cups cooked.

Country Bean Soup

Festive Cranberry Mold

· · · · ● ●

½ cup water
1 package (6 ounces) raspberry-flavored gelatin
1 can (8 ounces) cranberry sauce
1⅔ cups cranberry juice cocktail
1 cup sliced bananas (optional)
½ cup walnuts, toasted (optional)

In medium saucepan over medium-high heat, bring water to a boil. Add gelatin and stir until dissolved. Fold in cranberry sauce. Reduce heat to medium and cook until sauce is melted. Stir in cranberry juice cocktail.

Refrigerate mixture until slightly thickened. Fold in banana slices and walnuts, if desired. Pour mixture into 4-cup mold; cover and refrigerate until gelatin is set. *Makes 8 servings*

Minted Fruit Rice Salad

· · · · ● ●

⅔ cup DOLE® Pineapple Orange Juice or Pineapple Juice
⅓ cup water
1 cup uncooked instant rice
1 can (11 ounces) DOLE® Mandarin Oranges, drained
1 can (8 ounces) DOLE® Crushed Pineapple
½ cup chopped cucumber
⅓ cup chopped DOLE® Red Onion
3 tablespoons chopped fresh mint

• Combine juice and water in medium saucepan. Bring to a boil. Stir in rice. Remove from heat; cover, let stand 10 minutes.

• Stir together rice, drained mandarin oranges, undrained crushed pineapple, cucumber, onion and mint in medium serving bowl. Serve at room temperature or chilled. *Makes 4 servings*

Prep Time: 5 minutes
Cook Time: 15 minutes

Festive Cranberry Mold

Cranberry Salad

- 2 cups cranberries
- 1 cup water
- 1 cup EQUAL® SPOONFUL*
- 1 small package cranberry or cherry sugar-free gelatin
- 1 cup boiling water
- 1 cup diced celery
- 1 can (7¼ ounces) crushed pineapple, in juice
- ½ cup chopped walnuts

*May substitute 24 packets Equal® sweetener.

• Bring cranberries and 1 cup water to a boil. Remove from heat when cranberries have popped open. Add Equal® and stir. Set aside to cool.

• Dissolve gelatin with 1 cup boiling water. Add cranberry sauce; mix thoroughly. Add celery, pineapple with juice and walnuts. Pour into lightly greased mold or bowl. Place in refrigerator until set.

Makes 8 servings

Homestead Succotash

- ¼ pound bacon, diced
- 1 cup chopped onion
- ½ teaspoon dried thyme leaves
- 1 can (15¼ ounces) DEL MONTE® Whole Kernel Golden Sweet Corn, drained
- 1 can (15¼ ounces) DEL MONTE Green Lima Beans, drained

1. Cook bacon in skillet until crisp; drain. Add onion and thyme; cook until onion is tender.

2. Stir in vegetables and heat through.

Makes 6 to 8 servings

Prep and Cook Time: 13 minutes

Cucumber and Herb Dressing Mold

- **1 envelope unflavored gelatin**
- **1 cup boiling water**
- **1 cup pared, seeded and grated cucumber**
- **½ cup finely chopped celery**
- **¼ cup finely chopped radishes**
- **2 tablespoons finely chopped onion**
- **2 tablespoons chopped pimiento**
- **2 tablespoons finely chopped parsley**
- **1 cup prepared HIDDEN VALLEY® The Original Ranch® Dressing**
  Lettuce leaves

In small bowl, stir gelatin into boiling water until dissolved; refrigerate until partially set. Gently press cucumber between paper towels to remove excess moisture. In large bowl, combine cucumber with remaining vegetables and parsley; cover and refrigerate. Stir salad dressing into partially set gelatin. Fold in vegetable mixture and pour into 1-quart mold; refrigerate until set. To serve, unmold onto lettuce-lined plate.

Makes 4 to 6 servings

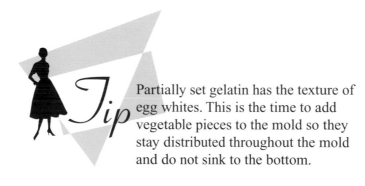

Tip

Partially set gelatin has the texture of egg whites. This is the time to add vegetable pieces to the mold so they stay distributed throughout the mold and do not sink to the bottom.

Campbell's® Green Bean Casserole

· · · ● ● ● ●

**1 can (10¾ ounces) CAMPBELL'S® Condensed Cream of
      Mushroom Soup *or* 98% Fat Free Cream of Mushroom Soup**
½ cup milk
1 teaspoon soy sauce
   Dash pepper
4 cups cooked cut green beans*
1 can (2.8 ounces) *French's*® French Fried Onions (1⅓ cups)

**Use 1 bag (16 to 20 ounces) frozen green beans, 2 packages (9 ounces each) frozen green
beans, 2 cans (about 16 ounces each) green beans or about 1½ pounds fresh green beans
for this recipe.*

1. In 1½-quart casserole mix soup, milk, soy sauce, pepper, beans and
½ *can* French Fried Onions.

2. Bake at 350°F. for 25 minutes or until hot.

3. Stir. Sprinkle remaining onions over bean mixture. Bake 5 minutes
more or until onions are golden.   ***Makes 6 servings***

Prep Time: 10 minutes
Cook Time: 30 minutes

Easy Pineapple Slaw

· · · ● ● ● ●

**1 can (15¼ ounces) DEL MONTE® Pineapple Tidbits
      In Its Own Juice**
⅓ cup mayonnaise
2 tablespoons vinegar
6 cups coleslaw mix or shredded cabbage

1. Drain pineapple, reserving 3 tablespoons juice.

2. Combine reserved juice, mayonnaise and vinegar; toss with pineapple
and coleslaw mix. Season with salt and pepper to taste, if desired.

Makes 4 to 6 servings

Prep Time: 5 minutes

Campbell's® Green Bean Casserole

Composed Fruit Salad with Chicken

2 cooked boneless, skinless chicken breast halves, sliced
1 can (8 ounces) DOLE® Pineapple Chunks, drained
½ DOLE® Papaya, peeled, seeded, sliced
2 small clusters seedless red grapes
2 tablespoons bottled poppy seed dressing
1 tablespoon lime juice
1 tablespoon minced cilantro

- Arrange chicken and fruit on plate.

- Combine salad dressing, lime juice and cilantro. Spoon dressing over chicken and fruit.   *Makes 2 servings*

Prep Time: 15 minutes

Apricot-Pineapple Mold

½ cup SMUCKER'S® Apricot Preserves
½ cup SMUCKER'S® Pineapple Topping
2 tablespoons vinegar
2½ cups water
1 teaspoon whole cloves
1 (4-inch) stick cinnamon
2 (3-ounce) packages orange-flavor gelatin
½ cup sour cream

In saucepan, combine preserves, pineapple topping, vinegar and water. Tie cloves and cinnamon in small square of cheesecloth and place in saucepan. Simmer mixture over low heat for 10 minutes. Remove spice bag.

Dissolve 1 package of gelatin in 2 cups of preserve mixture; stir until dissolved. Pour into a 6-cup mold and refrigerate until almost firm.

Meanwhile, dissolve remaining package of gelatin in remaining preserve mixture; stir until dissolved. Refrigerate until partially set. Beat with an electric mixer until fluffy. Fold in sour cream. Pour over first layer in mold. Refrigerate until firm, about 8 hours or overnight. Unmold to serve.   *Makes 8 to 10 serving*

Composed Fruit Salad with Chicken

Favorite Macaroni Salad

8 ounces uncooked medium shell pasta
⅓ cup reduced-fat sour cream
⅓ cup reduced-fat mayonnaise
⅓ cup *French's*® Bold n' Spicy Brown Mustard
1 tablespoon cider vinegar
3 cups bite-sized fresh vegetables, such as tomatoes, peppers, carrots and celery
¼ cup minced green onions

1. Cook pasta according to package directions using shortest cooking time; rinse with cold water and drain.

2. Combine sour cream, mayonnaise, mustard and vinegar in large bowl. Add pasta, vegetables and green onions. Toss gently to coat evenly. Season to taste with salt and pepper. Cover; chill in refrigerator 30 minutes. Stir before serving.   ***Makes 6 (1-cup) servings***

Prep Time: 20 minutes
Chill Time: 30 minutes

Note Create German-style mustard by adding minced garlic to French's® Zesty Deli Mustard.

Holiday Fruit Salad

3 packages (3 ounces each) strawberry gelatin
3 cups boiling water
2 ripe DOLE® Bananas
1 package (16 ounces) frozen strawberries
1 can (20 ounces) DOLE® Crushed Pineapple
1 package (8 ounces) cream cheese, softened
1 cup dairy sour cream or plain yogurt
¼ cup sugar
  Crisp DOLE® Lettuce leaves

• In large bowl, dissolve gelatin in boiling water. Slice bananas into gelatin mixture. Add frozen strawberries and undrained crushed pineapple. Reserve half of the mixture at room temperature. Pour remaining mixture into 13×9-inch pan. Refrigerate 1 hour or until firm.

• In mixer bowl, beat cream cheese with sour cream and sugar; spread over chilled layer. Gently spoon reserved gelatin mixture on top. Refrigerate until firm, about 2 hours.

• Cut into squares; serve on lettuce-lined salad plates. Garnish with additional pineapple and mint leaves, if desired.   *Makes 12 servings*

Tip
To unmold gelatin, dip the mold into a large bowl of warm water for about 10 seconds, immersing it almost to the rim. Cover the mold with a wet serving plate and invert. (The wet plate lets you slide the gelatin to the center.) Give the mold a gentle shake or two. If it does not slide out at once, return it to the bowl of water for a few seconds.

Classic Sides

Broccoli-Cheese Pilaf

• • • • ● ●

¼ **cup minced onion**
¼ **cup diced red bell pepper**
2 **cups instant rice**
1⅓ **cups water**
1 **can (10¾ ounces) condensed broccoli and cheese soup**
1 **tablespoon minced fresh parsley**
½ **teaspoon salt**

Lightly coat medium saucepan with nonstick cooking spray. Add onion and pepper; cook and stir until tender. Stir in rice; add water, soup, parsley and salt. Mix well. Bring to a boil. Reduce heat; cover and cook 10 minutes or until liquid is absorbed and rice is tender.

Makes 6 servings

Lawry's® Garlic Bread

• • • • ● ●

1 **loaf (1 pound) French or sourdough bread**
¼ **to ½ cup margarine**
2 **teaspoons LAWRY'S® Garlic Salt**

Slice bread in half lengthwise and score each half into 10 sections; do not cut through bottom crust. Spread margarine evenly on cut sides of bread halves. Evenly sprinkle Lawry's Garlic Salt over both halves. Broil for 2 to 3 minutes or until golden brown. To serve, finish cutting through bread slices with kitchen scissors. *Makes 20 slices*

Meal Idea: Serve with your favorite pasta, soup or entree and a crisp green salad. Also great prepared on French rolls and used with Italian sausage or smoked kielbasa sandwiches.

Variation: May use 1 teaspoon LAWRY'S® Garlic Powder With Parsley in place of Garlic Salt, if desired.

Prep Time: 5 minutes
Cook Time: 2 to 3 minutes

Classic Sides

Broccoli-Cheese Pilaf

Hickory-Flavored Baked Beans

- **4 slices bacon, cut into ½-inch pieces**
- **½ cup chopped onion**
- **1 can (28 ounces) baked beans**
- **½ cup hickory-flavored barbecue sauce**
- **2 tablespoons brown sugar**
- **1 teaspoon dry mustard**
- **¼ teaspoon hot pepper sauce (optional)**

Preheat oven to 350°F. In large oven-proof skillet, cook bacon and onion over medium-high heat until bacon is browned and crisp; drain fat. Add remaining ingredients; mix well. Bake, uncovered, 30 minutes or until hot and bubbly.   ***Makes 6 servings***

Serving Suggestion: Serve with simple picnic food like hot dogs or fancier fare such as grilled chicken or pork chops.

Hint: Set the skillet on a foil-lined baking sheet to catch the drips.

Strawberry Salad

- **2 packages (4-serving size each) strawberry-flavored gelatin**
- **1 cup boiling water**
- **2 packages (10 ounces each) frozen strawberries, thawed**
- **1 can (20 ounces) crushed pineapple, drained**
- **2 cups sour cream**

Combine gelatin and water in large bowl; stir until dissolved. Add strawberries and pineapple; mix well. Pour half of gelatin mixture into 13×9-inch pan. Refrigerate until set. Spread sour cream over gelatin in pan. Pour remaining gelatin mixture over sour cream. Refrigerate until ready to serve.   ***Makes 12 to 14 servings***

Hickory-Flavored Baked Beans

Tag-Along Fruit Salad

. . . ● ● ● ●

Citrus Dressing
- ¼ cup **CRISCO® Oil***
- ¼ cup **orange juice**
- 2 tablespoons **sugar**
- 2 tablespoons **lemon juice**
- ¼ teaspoon **paprika**

Salad
- 1 can (20 ounces) **pineapple chunks in juice, drained**
- 2 cups **seedless green grapes**
- 1¼ cups **miniature marshmallows****
- 1 cup **fresh orange sections**
- 1 cup **sliced fresh pears*****
- 1 cup **sliced banana*****
- 1 cup **sliced apples*****
- ½ cup **maraschino cherries, halved**

*Use your favorite Crisco Oil product.

**1 cup raisins can be substituted for marshmallows.

***Add Citrus Dressing to sliced apples, pears and bananas immediately after slicing to prevent discoloration.

1. For dressing, combine oil, orange juice, sugar, lemon juice and paprika in container with tight-fitting lid. Shake well.

2. Combine pineapple, grapes, marshmallows, oranges, pears, banana, apples and cherries in large bowl. Shake dressing. Pour over salad. Toss to coat. Cover. Refrigerate. Garnish, if desired.   ***Makes 10 servings***

Three-Bean Salad

1 (15½-ounce) can red kidney beans
1 (14½-ounce) can cut green beans
1 (14½-ounce) can yellow wax beans
1 green bell pepper, seeded and chopped
1 medium onion, chopped
2 ribs celery, sliced
¾ cup cider vinegar
⅓ cup **FILIPPO BERIO®** Olive Oil
2 tablespoons sugar
 Salt and freshly ground black pepper

Rinse and drain kidney beans; drain green and wax beans. In large bowl, combine beans, bell pepper, onion and celery. In small bowl, whisk together vinegar, olive oil and sugar. Pour over bean mixture; toss until lightly coated. Cover; refrigerate several hours or overnight before serving. Season to taste with salt and black pepper. Store salad, covered, in refrigerator up to 1 week. **Makes 10 to 12 servings**

Sauerkraut Salad

1 large can sauerkraut, drained
3 stalks celery, sliced
1 medium onion, diced
½ bell pepper, diced (any color)
½ cup pimiento, diced
⅓ cup vegetable oil
¼ cup white vinegar
¾ cup **EQUAL® SPOONFUL***
 Salt and pepper to taste

May substitute 18 packets Equal® sweetener.

• Combine sauerkraut, celery, onion, bell pepper and pimiento in large bowl. Mix together oil, vinegar and Equal® in separate container. Pour over salad; mix well. Season with salt and pepper to taste.

• Chill overnight or place in freezer for 20 minutes, stir and return to freezer for an additional 20 minutes. **Makes 10 servings**

Classic Sides

Confetti Rice Pilaf

1 tablespoon margarine or butter
1 cup uncooked regular or converted rice
1 cup fresh or drained canned sliced mushrooms
2 medium carrots, diced
1 envelope LIPTON® RECIPE SECRETS® Savory Herb with Garlic
   Soup Mix*
2¼ cups water

Also terrific with Lipton® Recipe Secrets® Golden Onion, Onion-Mushroom or Onion Soup Mix.

In 12-inch skillet, melt margarine over medium-high heat and cook rice, stirring frequently, until golden. Stir in mushrooms, carrots and Savory Herb with Garlic Soup Mix blended with water. Bring to a boil over high heat. Reduce heat to low and simmer covered 20 minutes or until rice is tender.   **Makes about 6 servings**

Pineapple Lime Mold

1 can (20 ounces) DOLE® Pineapple Chunks
2 packages (3 ounces each) lime gelatin
2 cups boiling water
1 cup sour cream
½ cup chopped walnuts
½ cup chopped DOLE® Celery

Drain pineapple chunks, reserve syrup. Dissolve gelatin in boiling water. Add sour cream and reserved syrup. Chill until slightly thickened. Stir in pineapple chunks, walnuts and celery. Pour into 7-cup mold. Chill until set.   **Makes 8 servings**

Confetti Rice Pilaf

Blueberry-Peach Salad

· · · · · ● ● ●

1 package (6 ounces) orange-flavored gelatin
⅓ cup sugar
1 teaspoon finely shredded orange peel
2¼ cups orange juice, divided
2 cups buttermilk
1 can (8 ounces) crushed pineapple, drained
1 cup chopped pitted halved peeled peaches
1 cup fresh or frozen unsweetened blueberries, thawed
1 carton (8 ounces) dairy sour cream

In medium saucepan combine gelatin and sugar; stir in orange peel and 2 cups orange juice. Cook and stir until gelatin is dissolved; cool. Stir in buttermilk. Refrigerate until partially set. Fold in fruit; spoon into 10 individual molds. Refrigerate 6 hours or until firm. Combine sour cream and remaining ¼ cup orange juice; refrigerate. Unmold salad; serve with sour cream mixture.   ***Makes 10 servings***

*Favorite recipe from **Wisconsin Milk Marketing Board***

Smoked Turkey & Fruit Salad

· · · · · ● ● ●

1 package (16 ounces) DOLE® Classic Iceberg Salad
1 can (11 ounces) DOLE® Mandarin Oranges, drained
4 ounces deli-sliced smoked turkey or chicken, cut into ½-inch
    slices
½ cup DOLE® Golden or Seedless Raisins
½ cup fat free or light ranch salad dressing
1 can (20 ounces) DOLE® Pineapple Slices, drained and cut
    in half

• Toss together salad, mandarin oranges, turkey and raisins in large bowl. Pour in dressing; toss well to evenly coat.

• Spoon salad onto large serving platter. Arrange halved pineapple slices around salad.   ***Makes 4 servings***

Prep Time: 15 minutes

Classic Sides

Blueberry-Peach Salad

Holiday Vegetable Bake

········

1 package (16 ounces) frozen vegetable combination
1 can (10¾ ounces) condensed cream of broccoli soup
⅓ cup milk
1⅓ cups *French's®* French Fried Onions, divided

Microwave Directions
Combine vegetables, soup, milk and ⅔ *cup* French Fried Onions in
2-quart microwavable casserole. Microwave,* uncovered, on HIGH 10 to
12 minutes or until vegetables are crisp-tender, stirring halfway through
cooking time. Sprinkle with remaining ⅔ *cup* onions. Microwave
1 minute or until onions are golden.   ***Makes 4 to 6 servings***

*Or, bake in preheated 375°F oven 30 to 35 minutes.

Prep Time: 5 minutes
Cook Time: 10 minutes

Garlic Onion Bread

········

½ cup butter or margarine, softened
2 tablespoons minced garlic
1 tablespoon chopped parsley
1 loaf (14 inches) Italian bread, split lengthwise in half
1⅓ cups *French's®* French Fried Onions
¼ cup grated Parmesan cheese

1. Preheat oven to 350°F. Mix butter, garlic and parsley. Spread half the
butter mixture onto each cut side of bread. Sprinkle each half with ⅔ *cup*
French Fried Onions and 2 tablespoons cheese.

2. Place bread on baking sheet. Bake 5 minutes or until hot and onions
are golden brown. Cut each half into 8 slices.   ***Makes 8 servings***

Tip: You may substitute ⅔ cup prepared pesto sauce for the butter mixture.

Prep Time: 10 minutes
Cook Time: 5 minutes

Holiday Vegetable Bake

Beet and Pear Salad

· · • • • •

1 can (15¼ ounces) DEL MONTE® Bartlett Pear Halves
1 can (14½ ounces) DEL MONTE Sliced Beets, drained
½ cup thinly sliced red onion, separated into rings
2 tablespoons vegetable oil
1 tablespoon white wine vinegar
⅓ cup crumbled blue cheese
  Lettuce leaves, optional

1. Drain pears reserving 1 tablespoon syrup.

2. Cut pears in half lengthwise.

3. Place pears, beets and onion in medium bowl.

4. Whisk together oil, vinegar and reserved syrup. Pour over salad; toss gently.

5. Just before serving, add cheese and toss. Serve on bed of lettuce leaves, if desired.   *Makes 4 to 6 servings*

Prep Time: 10 minutes

Ham and Navy Bean Soup

8 ounces dried navy beans, rinsed and drained
6 cups water
1 ham bone
1 medium yellow onion, chopped
2 ribs celery, finely chopped
2 bay leaves
1½ teaspoons dried tarragon leaves
1½ teaspoons salt
¼ teaspoon black pepper

Slow Cooker Directions

1. Place beans in large bowl; cover completely with water. Soak 6 to 8 hours or overnight. Drain beans; discard water.

2. Combine beans, 6 cups water, ham bone, onion, celery, bay leaves and tarragon in slow cooker. Cover; cook on LOW 8 hours or on HIGH 4 hours. Discard ham bone and bay leaves; stir in salt and pepper.

Makes 8 servings

Tip If you don't have a slow cooker, combine all the ingredients in step 2 in a Dutch oven. Cover and simmer 2 to 2½ hours until the beans are done.

In-Style Desserts

Rediscover fashionable '50s desserts—fruit cocktail cakes, delicious parfait-style puddings and pies, baked Alaska and more. Best of all, they're easy to make!

Brownie Baked Alaska

Brownie Baked Alaskas

2 purchased brownies (2½ inches square)
2 scoops fudge swirl ice cream (or favorite flavor)
⅓ cup semisweet chocolate chips
2 tablespoons light corn syrup or milk
2 egg whites
¼ cup sugar

1. Preheat oven to 500°F. Place brownies on small cookie sheet; top each with scoop of ice cream and place in freezer.

2. Melt chocolate chips in small saucepan over low heat. Stir in corn syrup; set aside and keep warm.

3. Beat egg whites to soft peaks in small bowl. Gradually beat in sugar; continue beating until stiff peaks form. Spread egg white mixture over ice cream and brownies with small spatula (ice cream and brownies should be completely covered with egg white mixture).

4. Bake 2 to 3 minutes or until meringue is golden. Spread chocolate sauce on serving plates; place baked Alaskas over sauce.

Makes 2 servings

Cranberry Crunch Gelatin

1 package (3 ounces) cherry-flavored gelatin mix, plus ingredients to prepare
1 can (16 ounces) whole cranberry sauce
1 cup miniature marshmallows
1 cup coarsely chopped English walnuts

Prepare gelatin according to package directions. Chill until slightly set, about 2 hours. Thoroughly fold in remaining ingredients. Chill until firm, about 2 to 3 hours.

Makes 6 servings

Pineapple Upside-Down Cake

Topping

- ½ **cup butter or margarine**
- 1 **cup firmly packed brown sugar**
- 1 **can (20 ounces) pineapple slices, well drained**
  Maraschino cherries, drained and halved
  Walnut halves

Cake

- 1 **package DUNCAN HINES® Moist Deluxe® Pineapple Supreme Cake Mix**
- 1 **package (4-serving size) vanilla-flavor instant pudding and pie filling mix**
- 4 **eggs**
- 1 **cup water**
- ½ **cup oil**

1. Preheat oven to 350°F.

2. For topping, melt butter over low heat in 12-inch cast-iron skillet or skillet with oven-proof handle. Remove from heat. Stir in brown sugar. Spread to cover bottom of skillet. Arrange pineapple slices, maraschino cherries and walnut halves in skillet. Set aside.

3. For cake, combine cake mix, pudding mix, eggs, water and oil in large mixing bowl. Beat at medium speed with electric mixer for 2 minutes. Pour batter evenly over fruit in skillet. Bake at 350°F for 1 hour or until toothpick inserted in center comes out clean. Invert onto serving plate.

Makes 16 to 20 servings

Tip Cake can be made in a 13×9×2-inch pan. Bake at 350°F for 45 to 55 minutes or until toothpick inserted in center comes out clean. Cake is also delicious using Duncan Hines® Moist Deluxe® Yellow Cake Mix.

In-Style Desserts

Pineapple Upside-Down Cake

Berry Delicious Trifles

- 1 package (4-serving size) instant vanilla pudding and pie filling mix
- 2¼ cups milk
- 1 cup sliced strawberries
- 1 cup raspberries
- 1 cup blueberries
- 1 frozen pound cake (10¾ ounces), thawed
- 2 tablespoons orange-flavored liqueur or orange juice
- ¼ cup orange marmalade
- Sweetened whipped cream and mint leaves (optional)

Beat pudding mix and milk in medium bowl with electric mixer at low speed 2 minutes; set aside. Combine strawberries, raspberries and blueberries in medium bowl; set aside.

Slice cake into 12 slices, each about ½-inch wide. Brush one side of each piece with liqueur; spread marmalade over liqueur.

Cut cake slices in half lengthwise. Place 4 pieces of cake each against side of 6 martini or parfait glasses with marmalade side toward center of glass.

Place ¼ cup berries in bottom of each glass; top each with heaping ⅓ cup pudding mix and then ¼ cup berries. Refrigerate 30 minutes. Garnish with sweetened whipped cream and mint leaves, if desired.

Makes 6 servings

Berry Delicious Trifle

Golden Chiffon Cake

5 **eggs, separated**
¼ **teaspoon cream of tartar**
2¼ **cups all-purpose flour**
1⅓ **cups sugar**
1 **tablespoon baking powder**
1 **teaspoon salt**
¾ **cup water**
½ **cup vegetable oil**
1 **teaspoon vanilla**
½ **teaspoon orange extract**
Fresh fruit and whipped cream for garnish

1. Preheat oven to 325°F.

2. Beat egg whites and cream of tartar in large bowl until stiff peaks form; set aside.

3. Sift flour, sugar, baking powder and salt into large bowl. Make a well in flour mixture. Add egg yolks, water, oil, vanilla and orange extract; mix well. Fold in egg white mixture.

4. Immediately spread in *ungreased* 10-inch tube pan. Bake 55 minutes. *Increase oven temperature to 350°F.* Continue baking 10 minutes or until cake springs back when lightly touched with finger. Invert pan and allow cake to cool completely before removing from pan. Garnish with fresh fruit and whipped cream, if desired. **Makes one 10-inch tube cake**

Golden Chiffon Cake

German Chocolate Cake

¼ cup HERSHEY'S Cocoa
½ cup boiling water
1 cup plus 3 tablespoons butter or margarine, softened
2¼ cups sugar
1 teaspoon vanilla extract
4 eggs
2 cups all-purpose flour
1 teaspoon baking soda
½ teaspoon salt
1 cup buttermilk or sour milk*
Coconut Pecan Frosting (recipe follows)
Pecan halves (optional)

*To sour milk: Use 1 tablespoon white vinegar plus milk to equal 1 cup.

Heat oven to 350°F. Grease and flour three 9-inch round baking pans. Combine cocoa and water in small bowl; stir until smooth. Set aside to cool. Beat butter, sugar and vanilla in large bowl until fluffy. Add eggs, one at a time, beating well after each addition. Stir together flour, baking soda and salt; add alternately with chocolate mixture and buttermilk to butter mixture. Mix only until smooth. Pour batter into prepared pans. Bake 25 to 30 minutes or until top springs back when touched lightly. Cool 5 minutes; remove from pans. Cool completely on wire rack. Prepare Coconut Pecan Frosting; spread between layers and over top. Garnish with pecan halves, if desired.   **Makes 10 to 12 servings**

Coconut Pecan Frosting

1 can (14 ounces) sweetened condensed milk
3 egg yolks, slightly beaten
½ cup butter or margarine
1 teaspoon vanilla extract
1⅓ cups MOUNDS® Sweetened Coconut Flakes
1 cup chopped pecans

Place sweetened condensed milk, egg yolks and butter in medium saucepan. Cook over low heat, stirring constantly, until mixture is thickened and bubbly. Remove from heat; stir in vanilla, coconut and pecans. Cool to room temperature.   **Makes about 2⅔ cups frosting**

German Chocolate Cake

Creamy Banana Pudding

· · ● ● ● ●

1 (14-ounce) can EAGLE BRAND® Sweetened Condensed Milk (NOT evaporated milk)
1½ cups cold water
1 (4-serving size) package instant vanilla pudding and pie filling mix
2 cups (1 pint) whipping cream, whipped
36 vanilla wafers
3 medium bananas, sliced and dipped in lemon juice from concentrate

1. In large mixing bowl, combine Eagle Brand and water. Add pudding mix; beat until well blended. Chill 5 minutes.

2. Fold in whipped cream. Spoon 1 cup pudding mixture into 2½-quart glass serving bowl.

3. Top with one-third each of vanilla wafers, bananas and pudding mixture. Repeat layering twice, ending with pudding mixture. Chill thoroughly. Garnish as desired. Refrigerate leftovers.

Makes 8 to 10 servings

Prep Time: 15 minutes

Tip Liven up desserts with a variety of garnishes. Use fresh fruit such as raspberries or sliced strawberries along with a sprig of fresh mint. Or, top with white and dark chocolate curls.

Creamy Banana Pudding

Carnation® Famous Fudge

- 1½ cups granulated sugar
- ⅔ cup (5 fluid-ounce can) NESTLÉ® CARNATION® Evaporated Milk
- 2 tablespoons butter or margarine
- ¼ teaspoon salt
- 2 cups miniature marshmallows
- 1½ cups (9 ounces) NESTLÉ® TOLL HOUSE® Semi-Sweet Chocolate Morsels
- ½ cup chopped pecans or walnuts (optional)
- 1 teaspoon vanilla extract

LINE 8-inch-square baking pan with foil.

COMBINE sugar, evaporated milk, butter and salt in medium, *heavy-duty* saucepan. Bring to a *full rolling boil* over medium heat, stirring constantly. Boil, stirring constantly, for 4 to 5 minutes. Remove from heat.

STIR in marshmallows, morsels, nuts and vanilla extract. Stir vigorously for 1 minute or until marshmallows are melted. Pour into prepared baking pan; refrigerate for 2 hours or until firm. Lift from pan; remove foil. Cut into pieces. **Makes about 49 pieces**

For Milk Chocolate Fudge: SUBSTITUTE *1¾ cups (11.5-ounce package) NESTLÉ® TOLL HOUSE® Milk Chocolate Morsels for Semi-Sweet Morsels.*

For Butterscotch Fudge: SUBSTITUTE *1⅔ cups (11-ounce package) NESTLÉ® TOLL HOUSE® Butterscotch Flavored Morsels for Semi-Sweet Morsels.*

For Peanutty Chocolate Fudge: SUBSTITUTE *1⅔ cups (11-ounce package) NESTLÉ® TOLL HOUSE® Peanut Butter & Milk Chocolate Morsels for Semi-Sweet Morsels and ½ cup chopped peanuts for pecans or walnuts.*

Pineapple Mousse Torte

Chocolate Crumb Crust (recipe follows)
1 package (8 ounces) cream cheese, softened
1¼ cups sugar
½ teaspoon grated lemon peel
1 can (15¼ ounces) DEL MONTE® Crushed Pineapple In Its Own Juice, undrained
1 can (8 ounces) DEL MONTE Pineapple Tidbits In Its Own Juice, undrained
2 envelopes unflavored gelatin
2¼ cups whipping cream, whipped

1. Prepare crumb crust; set aside.

2. Blend cream cheese with sugar and lemon peel.

3. Drain juice from crushed pineapple and tidbits into small saucepan. Sprinkle gelatin over juice. Place over low heat and stir until gelatin is completely dissolved.

4. Add crushed pineapple to cream cheese mixture; stir in gelatin mixture until blended. Thoroughly fold in whipped cream.

5. Pour filling into crust. Chill at least 5 hours or overnight. Remove sides of pan. Top with pineapple tidbits and garnish, if desired.

Makes 10 to 12 servings

Prep Time: 20 minutes
Chill Time: 5 hours

Chocolate Crumb Crust

1¾ cups chocolate wafer crumbs
½ cup butter or margarine, melted

Mix ingredients; press firmly onto bottom of 9-inch springform pan.

Orange Kiss Me Cake

1 large orange
1 cup raisins
⅔ cup chopped walnuts, divided
2 cups all-purpose flour
1⅓ cups sugar, divided
1 teaspoon baking soda
1 teaspoon salt
1 cup milk, divided
½ cup shortening
2 eggs
1 teaspoon ground cinnamon

1. Preheat oven to 350°F. Grease and flour 6 (4-inch) miniature Bundt pans or 1 (10-inch) Bundt pan.

2. Juice orange. Reserve ⅓ cup juice. Coarsely chop remaining orange pulp and peel. Process pulp, peel, raisins and ⅓ cup walnuts in food processor fitted with metal blade until finely ground.

3. Sift flour, 1 cup sugar, baking soda and salt together in large bowl. Add ¾ cup milk and shortening. Beat 2 minutes with electric mixer at medium speed until well blended. Beat 2 minutes more. Add eggs and remaining ¼ cup milk; beat 2 minutes. Fold orange mixture into batter; mix well. Pour into prepared pans.

4. Bake 40 to 45 minutes or until toothpick inserted near center comes out clean. Cool in pan 15 minutes. Invert onto serving plate. Poke holes in cakes with wooden skewer or fork tines.

5. Pour reserved juice over cakes. Combine remaining ⅓ cup sugar, ⅓ cup walnuts and cinnamon in small bowl. Sprinkle over cakes. Garnish as desired.

Makes 12 servings

Orange Kiss Me Cakes

Cold Cherry Mousse with Vanilla Sauce

1 envelope whipped topping mix
½ cup fat-free (skim) milk
½ teaspoon vanilla
2 envelopes unflavored gelatin
½ cup sugar
½ cup cold water
1 package (16 ounces) frozen unsweetened cherries, thawed, undrained and divided
1 tablespoon fresh lemon juice
½ teaspoon almond extract
Vanilla Sauce (recipe follows)

Prepare whipped topping according to package directions using milk and vanilla; set aside. Combine gelatin and sugar in small saucepan; stir in water. Let stand 5 minutes to soften. Heat over low heat until gelatin is completely dissolved. Cool to room temperature. Set aside 1 cup cherries without juice for garnish. Place remaining cherries and juice in blender. Add lemon juice, almond extract and gelatin mixture; process until blended. Fold cherry purée into whipped topping. Pour mixture into Bundt pan or ring mold. Refrigerate 4 hours or overnight until jelled.

To serve, unmold mousse onto large serving plate. Spoon remaining 1 cup cherries into center of mousse. Serve with Vanilla Sauce. Garnish with fresh mint, if desired. *Makes 6 servings*

Vanilla Sauce

4½ teaspoons cherry brandy *or* 1 teaspoon vanilla plus
½ teaspoon cherry extract
¾ cup melted vanilla ice milk or low-fat ice cream

Stir brandy into ice milk in small bowl; blend well. *Makes ¾ cup*

In-Style Desserts

Cold Cherry Mousse with Vanilla Sauce

Banana-Coconut Crunch Cake

Cake
1 package DUNCAN HINES® Moist Deluxe® Banana Supreme Cake Mix
1 package (4-serving size) banana-flavor instant pudding and pie filling mix
1 can (16 ounces) fruit cocktail, in juices, undrained
4 eggs
¼ cup vegetable oil
1 cup flaked coconut
½ cup chopped pecans
½ cup firmly packed brown sugar

Glaze
¾ cup granulated sugar
½ cup butter or margarine
½ cup evaporated milk
1⅓ cups flaked coconut

1. Preheat oven to 350°F. Grease and flour 13×9×2-inch pan.

2. For cake, combine cake mix, pudding mix, fruit cocktail with juice, eggs and oil in large bowl. Beat at medium speed with electric mixer for 4 minutes. Stir in 1 cup coconut. Pour into prepared pan. Combine pecans and brown sugar in small bowl. Stir until well mixed. Sprinkle over batter. Bake at 350°F for 45 to 50 minutes or until toothpick inserted in center comes out clean.

3. For glaze, combine granulated sugar, butter and evaporated milk in medium saucepan. Bring to a boil. Cook for 2 minutes, stirring occasionally. Remove from heat. Stir in 1⅓ cups coconut. Pour over warm cake. Serve warm or at room temperature.

Makes 12 to 16 servings

In-Style Desserts

Banana-Coconut Crunch Cake

Shamrock Parfaits

- 1 envelope unflavored gelatin
- ½ cup cold water
- ¾ cup sugar
- ½ cup HERSHEY'S Cocoa
- 1¼ cups evaporated nonfat milk
- 1 teaspoon vanilla extract
- 2 cups frozen light non-dairy whipped topping, thawed, divided
- ⅛ teaspoon mint extract
- 6 to 7 drops green food color

1. Sprinkle gelatin over water in medium bowl; let stand 2 minutes to soften. Cook over low heat, stirring constantly, until gelatin is completely dissolved, about 3 minutes. Stir together sugar and cocoa in small bowl; add gradually to gelatin mixture, stirring with whisk until well blended. Continue to cook over low heat, stirring constantly, until sugar is dissolved, about 3 minutes. Remove from heat. Stir in evaporated milk and vanilla. Pour mixture into large bowl. Refrigerate, stirring occasionally, until mixture mounds slightly when dropped from spoon, about 20 minutes.

2. Fold ½ cup whipped topping into chocolate mixture. Divide about half of mixture evenly among 8 parfait or wine glasses. Stir extract and food color into remaining 1½ cups topping; divide evenly among glasses. Spoon remaining chocolate mixture over topping in each glass. Garnish as desired. Serve immediately or cover and refrigerate until serving time.

Makes 8 servings

Shamrock Parfaits

Chocolate Orange Marble Chiffon Cake

⅓ cup **HERSHEY'S Cocoa**
¼ **cup hot water**
3 **tablespoons plus 1½ cups sugar, divided**
2 **tablespoons plus ½ cup vegetable oil, divided**
2¼ **cups all-purpose flour**
1 **tablespoon baking powder**
1 **teaspoon salt**
¾ **cup cold water**
7 **egg yolks**
1 **cup egg whites (about 8)**
½ **teaspoon cream of tartar**
1 **tablespoon freshly grated orange peel**
Orange Glaze (page 210)

1. Remove top oven rack; move other rack to lowest position. Heat oven to 325°F.

2. Stir together cocoa and hot water in medium bowl. Stir in 3 tablespoons sugar and 2 tablespoons oil; set aside. Stir together flour, remaining 1½ cups sugar, baking powder and salt in large bowl. Add cold water, remaining ½ cup oil and egg yolks; beat with spoon until smooth.

3. Beat egg whites and cream of tartar in another large bowl on high speed of mixer until stiff peaks form. Pour egg yolk mixture in a thin stream over egg white mixture, gently folding just until blended. Remove 2 cups batter; add to chocolate mixture, gently folding until well blended. Fold orange peel into remaining batter.

4. Spoon half the orange batter into ungreased 10-inch tube pan; drop half the chocolate batter on top by spoonfuls. Repeat layers of orange and chocolate batters. Gently swirl with knife for marbled effect, leaving definite orange and chocolate areas.

5. Bake 1 hour and 15 to 20 minutes or until top springs back when lightly touched. Immediately invert cake pan onto heatproof funnel; cool cake completely. Remove cake from pan; invert onto serving plate. Prepare Orange Glaze; spread over top of cake, allowing glaze to run down sides. Garnish as desired. ***Makes 12 to 16 servings***

continued on page 210

In-Style Desserts

Chocolate Orange Marble Chiffon Cake

Orange Glaze

⅓ cup butter
2 cups powdered sugar
2 tablespoons orange juice
½ teaspoon freshly grated orange peel

Melt butter in medium saucepan over low heat. Remove from heat; gradually stir in powdered sugar, orange juice and orange peel, beating until smooth and of desired consistency. Add additional orange juice, 1 teaspoon at a time, if needed.   ***Makes about 1½ cups glaze***

Almond-Pumpkin Chiffon Pudding

1 envelope unflavored gelatin
1 cup 1% low-fat milk
1 cup solid pack pumpkin
½ teaspoon pumpkin pie spice
1 container (8 ounces) plain low-fat yogurt
3 egg whites
   Dash salt
⅔ cup packed brown sugar
½ cup chopped toasted California Almonds, divided

Sprinkle gelatin over milk in small saucepan; let stand 5 minutes to soften. Cook and stir constantly over low heat until gelatin dissolves; remove from heat. Stir in pumpkin and pumpkin pie spice. Cool to room temperature; stir in yogurt. Refrigerate until mixture begins to thicken and gel. Beat egg whites with salt to form soft peaks. Gradually beat in brown sugar, beating to form stiff peaks; fold into pumpkin mixture. Sprinkle 1 tablespoon almonds over bottom of greased 6-cup mold. Fold remaining almonds into pumpkin mixture; spoon into mold. Refrigerate until firm. Unmold to serve.   ***Makes 8 servings***

*Favorite recipe from **Almond Board of California***

Almond-Pumpkin Chiffon Pudding

Sweetheart Pudding Parfaits

· · · • • • •

1 box (3.4 ounces) vanilla-flavored instant pudding mix
2 cups milk
2 cups coarsely chopped chocolate-covered mint cookies or
  chocolate sandwich cookies
¾ cup thawed frozen nondairy whipped topping
¼ cup strawberry, chocolate or caramel sundae topping, divided

1. Place 4 (10- to 12-ounce) parfait or stemmed glasses in freezer. Prepare pudding mix according to package directions with milk.

2. Layer ¼ cup cookies, ¼ cup pudding, 2 tablespoons whipped topping and 2 teaspoons sundae topping in each chilled glass. Spread layers evenly. Add second layer of cookies and pudding.

3. Top with remaining whipped topping and sundae topping. Garnish as desired.   ***Makes 4 servings***

Prep and Cook Time: 15 minutes

Lemon Chiffon

· · · • • • •

2 packages (4-serving size each) vanilla-flavored instant
  pudding mix
2 packages (4-serving size each) lemon-flavored gelatin
3 cups boiling water
1 container (8 ounces) frozen whipped topping, thawed

1. Combine pudding mix and gelatin in 5-quart serving bowl. Add boiling water, whisking constantly to dissolve completely. Refrigerate until mixture cools and thickens slightly, about 1 hour.

2. Stir in whipped topping and chill until mixture sets, at least 1 hour.
                              Makes 12 servings

In-Style Desserts

Sweetheart Pudding Parfaits

Delicate White Chocolate Cake

1 package DUNCAN HINES® Moist Deluxe® White Cake Mix
1 package (4-serving size) vanilla-flavor instant pudding and pie
   filling mix
4 egg whites
1 cup water
½ cup vegetable oil
5 ounces finely chopped white chocolate
1 cup cherry preserves
8 drops red food coloring (optional)
2 cups whipping cream, chilled
2 tablespoons confectioners' sugar
   Maraschino cherries for garnish
1 ounce white chocolate shavings for garnish

1. Preheat oven to 350°F. Cut waxed paper circles to fit bottoms of three 9-inch round cake pans. Grease bottoms and sides of pans. Line with waxed paper circles.

2. Combine cake mix, pudding mix, egg whites, water and oil in large mixing bowl. Beat at medium speed with electric mixer for 2 minutes. Fold in chopped white chocolate. Pour into prepared pans. Bake at 350°F for 18 to 22 minutes or until toothpick inserted into centers comes out clean. Cool in pans 15 minutes. Invert onto cooling racks. Peel off waxed paper. Cool completely.

3. Combine cherry preserves and food coloring, if desired. Stir to blend color.

4. Beat whipping cream in large bowl until soft peaks form. Add sugar gradually. Beat until stiff peaks form.

5. To assemble, place one cake layer on serving plate. Spread ½ cup cherry preserves over cake. Place second cake layer on top. Spread with remaining preserves. Place third cake layer on top. Frost sides and top of cake with whipped cream. Decorate with maraschino cherries and white chocolate shavings. Refrigerate until ready to serve.

Makes 12 to 16 servings

Delicate White Chocolate Cake

Ambrosia

1 can (20 ounces) DOLE® Pineapple Chunks
1 can (11 or 15 ounces) DOLE® Mandarin Oranges
1 firm, large DOLE® Banana, sliced (optional)
1½ cups DOLE® Seedless Grapes
1 cup miniature marshmallows
1 cup flaked coconut
½ cup pecan halves or coarsely chopped nuts
1 cup vanilla yogurt or sour cream
1 tablespoon brown sugar

• Drain pineapple chunks and mandarin oranges. In large bowl, combine pineapple chunks, mandarin oranges, banana, grapes, marshmallows, coconut and nuts. In 1-quart measure, combine yogurt and brown sugar. Stir into fruit mixture. Refrigerate, covered, 1 hour or overnight.

Makes 4 servings

Fruit Cocktail Cake

2 cups all-purpose flour
2 cups fruit cocktail, drained
1¾ cups sugar
½ cup butter, melted
2 eggs
2 teaspoons baking soda
½ teaspoon salt

Preheat oven to 350°F. Grease 13×9-inch baking pan. Set aside. Combine all ingredients in large bowl. Pour into prepared pan. Bake 40 minutes or until toothpick inserted into center comes out clean.

Makes 10 to 12 servings

Strawberry Bavarian Deluxe

½ **bag whole frozen unsweetened strawberries**
    (1 mounded quart), partially thawed
¼ **cup granular sucralose**
¼ **cup low-sugar strawberry preserves**
 2 **tablespoons balsamic vinegar**
¾ **cup water, divided**
 2 **envelopes (¼ ounce each) unflavored gelatin**
 1 **tablespoon honey**
½ **cup pasteurized liquid egg whites**
½ **teaspoon cream of tartar**
 1 **pint strawberries, washed, dried and hulled**
 1 **cup thawed frozen light whipped topping**

1. Place strawberries, sucralose and preserves in bowl of food processor fitted with chopping blade. Process until smooth. Transfer mixture to bowl. Set aside.

2. Combine vinegar and ¼ cup water in small saucepan. Sprinkle in gelatin and let stand until softened. Add remaining ½ cup of water to pan along with honey; stir to mix. Cook over medium heat, stirring, until gelatin dissolves. Whisk gelatin mixture into berry mixture in bowl. Refrigerate, covered, until mixture is slightly set.

3. Meanwhile, combine liquid egg whites and cream of tartar in bowl. When berry-gelatin mixture is soupy, whip egg whites until tripled in volume and at soft peak stage. Gently fold egg whites, ⅓ at a time, into chilled berry-gelatin mixture, being careful not to deflate egg whites. Fold until mixture is uniform in color. Scrape mousse into prechilled 2-quart mold, such as a nonstick Bundt pan. Refrigerate covered for at least 8 hours or overnight.

4. To serve, run tip of knife around top of mold, inside rim and center (if using Bundt pan). Dip mold briefly into large bowl of hot water to loosen mousse, lifting occasionally and shaking gently to see if mousse is released. To unmold, center a flat serving plate on top of the mold, hold firmly so mold doesn't shift, and invert plate and mold. Shake gently to release. Remove mold; refrigerate. After 10 to 15 minutes, remove from refrigerator. Cut into wedges; garnish with strawberries and whipped topping. ***Makes 10 servings***

In-Style Desserts

The publisher would like to thank the companies and organizations listed below for the use of their recipes and photographs in this publication.

Almond Board of California

Bays English Muffin Corporation

Birds Eye®

Bob Evans®

Butterball® Turkey

Campbell Soup Company

ConAgra Foods®

Del Monte Corporation

Dole Food Company, Inc.

Duncan Hines® and Moist Deluxe® are registered trademarks of Aurora Foods Inc.

Eagle Brand®

Equal® sweetener

Filippo Berio® Olive Oil

Fleischmann's® Margarines and Spreads

Florida Department of Agriculture and Consumer Services, Bureau of Seafood and Aquaculture

The Golden Grain Company®

Hebrew National®

Heinz North America

Hershey Foods Corporation

The Hidden Valley® Food Products Company

Hillshire Farm®

Hormel Foods, LLC

The Kingsford Products Company

Lawry's® Foods

McIlhenny Company (TABASCO® brand Pepper Sauce)

Mott's® is a registered trademark of Mott's, Inc.

National Pork Board

Nestlé USA

Newman's Own, Inc.®

Reckitt Benckiser Inc.

The J.M. Smucker Company

StarKist® Seafood Company

Unilever Bestfoods North America

Veg•All®

Wisconsin Milk Marketing Board

Acknowledgments

Index

Index

Index

Index

METRIC CONVERSION CHART

VOLUME MEASUREMENTS (dry)

$1/8$ teaspoon = 0.5 mL
$1/4$ teaspoon = 1 mL
$1/2$ teaspoon = 2 mL
$3/4$ teaspoon = 4 mL
1 teaspoon = 5 mL
1 tablespoon = 15 mL
2 tablespoons = 30 mL
$1/4$ cup = 60 mL
$1/3$ cup = 75 mL
$1/2$ cup = 125 mL
$2/3$ cup = 150 mL
$3/4$ cup = 175 mL
1 cup = 250 mL
2 cups = 1 pint = 500 mL
3 cups = 750 mL
4 cups = 1 quart = 1 L

VOLUME MEASUREMENTS (fluid)

1 fluid ounce (2 tablespoons) = 30 mL
4 fluid ounces ($1/2$ cup) = 125 mL
8 fluid ounces (1 cup) = 250 mL
12 fluid ounces ($1 1/2$ cups) = 375 mL
16 fluid ounces (2 cups) = 500 mL

WEIGHTS (mass)

$1/2$ ounce = 15 g
1 ounce = 30 g
3 ounces = 90 g
4 ounces = 120 g
8 ounces = 225 g
10 ounces = 285 g
12 ounces = 360 g
16 ounces = 1 pound = 450 g

DIMENSIONS

$1/16$ inch = 2 mm
$1/8$ inch = 3 mm
$1/4$ inch = 6 mm
$1/2$ inch = 1.5 cm
$3/4$ inch = 2 cm
1 inch = 2.5 cm

OVEN TEMPERATURES

250°F = 120°C
275°F = 140°C
300°F = 150°C
325°F = 160°C
350°F = 180°C
375°F = 190°C
400°F = 200°C
425°F = 220°C
450°F = 230°C

BAKING PAN SIZES

Utensil	Size in Inches/Quarts	Metric Volume	Size in Centimeters
Baking or Cake Pan (square or rectangular)	$8 \times 8 \times 2$	2 L	$20 \times 20 \times 5$
	$9 \times 9 \times 2$	2.5 L	$23 \times 23 \times 5$
	$12 \times 8 \times 2$	3 L	$30 \times 20 \times 5$
	$13 \times 9 \times 2$	3.5 L	$33 \times 23 \times 5$
Loaf Pan	$8 \times 4 \times 3$	1.5 L	$20 \times 10 \times 7$
	$9 \times 5 \times 3$	2 L	$23 \times 13 \times 7$
Round Layer Cake Pan	$8 \times 1 1/2$	1.2 L	20×4
	$9 \times 1 1/2$	1.5 L	23×4
Pie Plate	$8 \times 1 1/4$	750 mL	20×3
	$9 \times 1 1/4$	1 L	23×3
Baking Dish or Casserole	1 quart	1 L	—
	$1 1/2$ quart	1.5 L	—
	2 quart	2 L	—

Metric Chart